THE NATURAL HISTORY OF ATHEISM

THE NATURAL HISTORY OF ATHEISM

JOHN STUART BLACKIE

GYAN

Published by

Gyan Publishing House
5, Ansari Road
Daryaganj, New Delhi-110002
Phone: 011-47034999, 9811692060
E-mail: books@gyanbooks.com

Distribution Network
gyanbooks.com
India, USA, Canada, UK, Australia, France

ISBN: 978-81-212-9132-3 (PB)
First Published, 1878

2nd Impression 2023

Printed at: Gyan Press, Delhi.

THE NATURAL HISTORY OF ATHEISM
AUTHOR: JOHN STUART BLACKIE

THE NATURAL HISTORY OF ATHEISM.

THE NATURAL HISTORY OF ATHEISM

BY

JOHN STUART BLACKIE

PROFESSOR OF GREEK AT THE UNIVERSITY OF EDINBURGH

"Mala et impia est consuetudo contra deos disputandi, sive ex animo id fit, sive simulate."—CICERO.

NEW YORK
SCRIBNER, ARMSTRONG & COMPANY
1878

CONTENTS.

CHAPTER I.

PRESUMPTIONS.

Πάντες τε θεῶν χατέουσ' ἄνθρωποι.

HESIOD.

Τίνος γὰρ ἄλλου ζώου ψυχὴ θεῶν τῶν τὰ μέγιστα καὶ κάλλιστα συνταξάντων ᾔσθηται ὅτι εἰσί; τί δὲ φῦλον ἄλλοι ἢ ἄνθρωποι θεοὺς θεραπεύουσι.

SOCRATES.

I REMEMBER well, when I was passing from boyhood into youth, some fifty years ago, shortly after the battle of Waterloo, there was a general conviction in the public mind—at least in that large section of the public which is more mightily stirred by the present than taught by the past—that after so many years' wild turmoil of guns and bayonets, there was now an end forever of that culmination of sanguinary horror called War; and I remember no less distinctly how when, a few years afterwards, by the advice of a stout old doctor of divinity in Marischal College, Aberdeen,

I waded my way through that most interesting of all ancient theological treatises, "Cicero de Naturâ Deorum," and had finished the perusal with the abiding belief that that culmination of all speculative absurdities called Atheism was a thing of the past, and could no more reappear on the stage of credible things than those old women suspected of holding communion with the Evil One, who, not more than two hundred years ago, used to be flung into the milldam, to the effect that, if they were not witches they might sink, and if they were witches they might float and be burnt. But I have lived long enough now to understand that both these anticipations were premature. As for war, I have long since made up my mind that it is not only a theatre of horrors, but a school of virtue; and that in a rich and various world, crowded with antagonistic tendencies and contrary interests, hostile collisions of various kinds must take place; and the only thing to be done with war, by sensible men, is not to dream it out of the world, but, while we are never eager for it, to be always ready, and, when we are in the heat of the strife, to fight like men, and not like tigers. As for Atheism, again, I have learnt equally, by the consideration of certain recent phases of thought, taken along with the general history of human speculation, that it is a disease of the speculative faculty which must be expected to reappear from time to time, when men are shaken out of the firm forms of their old beliefs, and have not yet had time to work themselves into the well-defined mould of a new one. It indicates, in fact, a chaotic state of mind analogous to that physical chaos which makes its epiphany betwixt the destruction of an old world and the creation of a new.

What is Atheism? As a theory, with regard to the nature and constitution of the universe, the word means either that the mighty something, the τὸ πᾶν, the *all*, was produced out of nothing, nobody knows how, and goes on producing itself into something, nobody knows how; or that it has existed forever, and will exist forever, as a mighty confused complex of something that acts, called *force*, and something that is acted on, called *matter*; but it takes its shape from no intelligent or designing cause, merely from blind *chance*; or at least that it is a self-existent combination of forces and the results of forces, of which, in their unity, no intelligible account can be given.

Now the first observation that occurs to one on this view of the constitution of this wonderful structure of things called the world, is, that on the broad view of the ages and cycles of human speculation it is a strikingly exceptive, abnormal, and monstrous type of reasonable thought. It seems, on the first blush of the matter, to bear somewhat the same proportion to the general current of human thinking that dypsomania and other odd conditions of morbid sensibility do to the normal state of the human nerves. Or, to take another simile: the general aspect of the fields and the forests and the face of the earth, except in the desert of Sahara, is green; but sometimes, wandering in the depths of the leafy dells, or through the luxuriant beds of artificial gardens, we stumble on a single plant whose leaves are red, while all its congeners are of the normal green. This peculiar hue, though it have a certain novel attraction about it, is in fact a disease, and will not be looked on with favour by any gardener. Such exactly seems to be the case with Atheism. It is a doctrine so averse from the general current of human sentiment, that the unsophisticated mass of mankind instinctively turn away from it, as the other foxes did from that vulpine brother who, having lost his tail in a trap, tried to convince the whole world of foxes that the bushy appendage in the posterior region was a deformity of which all high-minded members of the vulpine aristocracy should get rid as soon as possible. In common times and under normal circumstances, men are not disposed to accept Atheism, in any shape, as having any positive value. It is simply a defect in the reason, as much as the want of an eyeball in what looks like an eye, or the want of a beard in what looks like a man. Men without beards, or women with them, will justly not be taken account of in the general estimate of the sexes.

The fact is, as Socrates says in the "Memorabilia," man is naturally and differentially a religious animal, and is not thoroughly or normally himself, unless when he is so. It has been so much the fashion lately to hunt out and to parade points of identity between man and the lower animals, that it may be a service to sound reason just to state the immense gap that exist betwixt the strange unfeathered biped called man and our first cousin the ape, if Dr. Darwin and Mr. Huxley will have it so. What monkey ever wrote an epic poem, or composed a tragedy or a comedy, or even a sonnet? What monkey professed his belief in any thirty-nine articles, or well-compacted Calvinistic confession, or gave in his adhesion to any Church, established or disestablished? Did any monkey ever smile or laugh (for a grin is not a laugh), or sing, or give the slightest indication of knowing even the most elementary propositions in the first six books of Euclid, such as are easily crammed into the head of the dullest undergraduate of the term? Plainly not. And though men in Egypt, for some symbolical reason that may not have been so foolish as we imagine, paid certain sacrosanct attentions and pious ministrations to crocodiles, there is no proof that crocodiles or monkeys, or any other of the lower animals, ever worshipped anybody. Dogs worship men, you will say. Yes, but only in a fashion. Dogs have neither churches nor creeds; and as the god whom they worship is the man who visibly feeds them and tangibly flogs them, it is a very cheap sort of religion. Socrates was certainly right in this matter, rather than Darwin. He saw as great a gap betwixt man and the lower animals in the descending scale, as betwixt men and the gods in the ascending scale; and he recognised the peculiar differential excellence of the human species simply in this, that they could recognise the gods, and give evidence of the recognition by the reverential observances of what we call a religion. Surely this was a much more human, more normal, and more noble way of philosophizing than to take infinite pains, as some of our modern scientific men do, on the one hand, to restore our lost brotherhood with the baboon, and, on the other, to raise up an impassable wall of partition between all reasonable creatures and the Supreme Reason from whom all creatures flow. We miscalculate very much indeed if we imagine that the peculiar doctrines and favourite fancies of a few cultivators of physical science in this small corner of the world, and in this small half of a century, are likely to exercise any notable influence over the thoughts of men, after the one-sided impulse out of which they arose shall have spent its force. Not only all the unsophisticated masses of men, but all the great originators of philosophic schools and the founders of churches, have been theists. Moses, David, and Solomon; Pythagoras, and Anaxagoras; Socrates, Plato, Aristotle, and Zeno; St. Paul and St. Peter; Mahomet, St. Bernard, Thomas Aquinas, Dante, Kepler, Copernicus, Shakespeare, Luther, Spinoza, Bacon, Leibnitz, Newton, Locke, Des Cartes, Kant, Hegel. Against such an array of great witnesses of sound human reason, it is only the narrowness of local conceit, or the madness of partisanship, that could plant such names as David Hume (if David Hume did indeed believe in his own bepuzzlements), Jeremy Bentham, and John Stuart Mill. As for Confucius and Buddha, the two great prophets of the far East, who certainly embrace a much wider sphere of human discipleship than any of our English sophists of the negative school, they lie outside of our Western European culture altogether; but in so far as they seem to have taught a morality without religion, or a religion without God, we shall say a word or two about them by-and-by.

That the general consent of the most cultivated part of the human race, taken in the gross, is in favour of theism, and against atheism, seems, therefore, as a fact, plain enough. But whether there be certain races of human beings, up in the frozen North, or down in the fervid South, the tablets of whose inner nature, when nicely read, present absolutely no traces of a recognition of a superior world-controlling power, this is a question by no means easy in an exhaustive way to answer. One of the speakers in Cicero's book above-named, starts precisely this question—"Whence," says he, "do you—*i.e.* the Stoics, who argue from the consent of the human race—prove the opinions of all nations? I verily believe that there are many people so lost in savagery that they have not even the slightest suspicion of the existence of gods."* Here are two contrary opinions: the one that there is a universal consent of all men and all peoples in the belief of a Supreme Being or Beings; the other, that there are nations so sunk in savagery, that they entertain not the remotest suspicion of God any more than their cattle, their sheep, or their swine; and to make these adverse notions more than opinions, to turn them into knowledge, as Plato is fond of saying, it is manifest that what we want is facts. Now the facts in this case are to be sought in remote and little travelled places, under circumstances not without danger, and, what is worse, often discouraging and disgusting to civilised men. Who is to go and live among wild men of the woods and roving Nomads of the waste for years, till he has thoroughly mastered their language, and by this process acquired the key to their notions and sentiments and convictions about whatever lies behind and above and within that wonderful evolution of beauty and grandeur and power, which we call the world? We naturally look to Christian missionaries here in the first place. They alone, with very few exceptions, seem to possess the earnestness of pur-

* "De Naturâ Deorum," i. 23.

pose, the single-hearted devotedness, and the intensity of moral apostleship, which could lead civilised men to make a moral experiment of this kind. But even their evidence in such a matter must be looked on with caution, and sifted with care. An intense zeal—without which a missionary would be nothing—so far from implying an impartial judgment in all moral and religious matters, not seldom renders such a judgment impossible. We may say generally, indeed, that a zealous Christian missionary is not the man fully to appreciate the amount of genuine theistic piety that may lie hidden and half choked beneath the grotesque mummeries and disgusting practices that are all that certain low types of humanity have to show for religion. It is not at all uncommon, even among ourselves, to hear persons and parties branded as atheistical, only because the individuals who so stigmatize them have not been able, and, perhaps, are not in the least willing, to appreciate the sort of theism which they profess. If Spinoza has been called an atheist, though he did not deny God, but rather denied the world, and was, therefore, as Hegel says, more properly styled an *acosmist;* how much more may many savage tribes have been termed atheistical by ignorant and unthinking missionaries who failed to make the very obvious distinction between worshipping gods who are no gods, and worshipping no god at all? With this caution, therefore, let us hear what the most intelligent of the missionaries have to say; and in such a case there are few men who have a better right to be called into court than the noble apostle of South Africa, Dr. Moffat. Here is a well-known passage about the African Bushmen:—"Hard is the Bushman's lot—friendless, forsaken, an outcast from the world; greatly preferring the company of the beasts of prey to that of civilised man. His gorah * soothes some solitary hours, although its sounds are often responded to by the lion's roar or the hyena's howl. He knows no God, knows nothing of eternity, yet dreads death, and has no shrine at which to leave his care and sorrows. We can scarcely conceive of human beings descending lower in the scale of ignorance and vice, while yet there can be no question that they are children of one common parent with ourselves." † And to the same effect is

* "The gorah is an instrument something like the bow of a violin—rather more curved—along which is stretched a catgut, to which is attached a small piece of quill. The player takes the quill in his mouth, and by strong inspirations and respirations produces a few soft notes in the vibrations of the catgut."

† "Missionary Labours and Scenes in South Africa," Thirtieth thousand, p. 15.

the distinct testimony of Dr. Monat in reference to the Andaman islanders :—"They have no conception of a Supreme Being. They have never risen from the effects they see around them, even to the most imperfect notion of a cause. They have never ascended in thought from the works to a Creator, or even to many Creators—that is to say, Polytheism."* And one of the most eminent investigators into the primitive condition of man has the following interesting passage :—"The opinion that religion is general and universal has been entertained by many high authorities. Yet it is opposed to the evidence of numerous trustworthy observers. Sailors, traders, and philosophers, Roman Catholic priests and Protestant missionaries, in ancient and in modern times, in every part of the globe, have concurred in stating that there are races of men altogether devoid of religion. The case is the stronger because in several instances the fact has greatly surprised him who records it, and has been entirely in opposition to all his preconceived views. On the other hand, it must be confessed that in some cases travellers denied the existence of religion merely because the tenets were unlike ours. The question

* "Adventures and Researches among the Andaman Islanders." By Frederick T. Monat, M.D., F.R.C.S. London. 1863. P. 303.

as to the general existence of religion among men is indeed to a great extent a matter of definition. If the mere sensation of fear, and the recognition that there are probably other beings more powerful than one's self, are sufficient alone to constitute a religion, then we must, I think, admit that religion is general to the human race. But when a child dreads the darkness, or shrinks from a lightless room, we never regard that as an evidence of religion. Moreover, if this definition be adopted, we cannot longer regard religion as peculiar to man. We must admit that the feeling of a dog or a horse towards his master is of the same character; and the baying of a dog to the moon is as much an act of worship as some ceremonies which have been so described by travellers." *

But strong as these testimonies appear, it is extremely doubtful how far they would satisfy an impartial jury impannelled to try the point we are now discussing. Certainly if anthropological questions of this kind are to be decided on the same strictness of detailed testimony that pecuniary cases are decided in our law courts, the three testimonies here given, notwithstanding the weight

* "Origin of Civilisation and Primitive Condition of Man." By Sir T. Lubbock. Pp. 138—9.

justly attributable to the words of the writers, would require to be submitted to the most sifting cross-examination before they could be accepted as elements in the formation of any conclusive verdict on the subject. And accordingly we find that another writer of equal authority, after quoting various testimonies in favour of the existence of atheistic races, nevertheless declares his opinion that no evidence sufficiently detailed and searching has been brought forward, such as might enable a cautious thinker to assert with confidence that there exists anywhere a race of human beings absolutely without religion of any kind.* And our great African explorer, Livingstone, talking of some of the most degraded tribes of the Africans with whom he came into connection, says, "There is no necessity for beginning to tell the most degraded of these people (the Bechuanas) of the existence of a God, or of the future state, the facts being universally admitted. Everything that cannot be accounted for by common causes is ascribed to the Deity—as creation, sudden death, &c. 'How curiously God made these things!' is a common expression, as is 'He was not killed by disease, he was killed by God.' And while speak-

* Tylor, "Primitive Culture," vol. i. p. 379.

ing of the departed—though there is nought in the physical appearance of the dead to justify the expression—they say, 'He has gone to the gods,' the phrase being identical with *abiit ad patres*." *

This testimony is sufficiently strong, but of course it is strong only within the range of personal observation which it includes, and does not necessarily contradict the assertion of Moffat; for Livingstone, in the very next page, honestly states that "he had not had any intercourse with either Caffre or Bushmen in their own tongue." On the whole, therefore, so far as our very imperfect evidence goes, we seem justified in concluding that, while some sort of religion seems to belong to man as man, one type of religion may differ from another as far as lust differs from love, opinion from knowledge, or caricature from art.† And, if there be races of reasonable beings who have no idea of a cause, it is just the same thing as if we were to find in every Alpine valley whole races of Cretins, or anywhere in the world whole races of idiots; they are defective creatures such as no

* "Livingstone's Missionary Travels," chap. viii. p. 158.

† An extremely interesting account of a very low type of religion, among the Ostjaks of Asiatic Russia, will be found in Alexander Castren's "Reise Erinnerungen," Petersburg, 1853, p. 288.

naturalist would receive into his normal description of one of Nature's types; such as roses, for instance, without fragrance, horses without hoofs, and birds without wings. Any type of things, indeed, as well as man, may by a combination of untoward influences, be curtailed and stunted into any sort of degradation.

So much for the facts. We return to our original assertion, and say, The great majority of human beings acknowledge God, and the practical form which this acknowledgment takes is called Religion. But this, no doubt, is a very wide and a very vague word, and requires exposition. In the main, however, its variations fall under two heads. Either it is a simple acknowledgment of an existing supreme authority in the universal order of things both physical and moral; or it contains further a philosophical theory with regard to the original creation and the continued preservation of the universe. Of these two types of popular faith the first is certainly the more important, affecting as it does directly the conduct of human life, and the position of personal subordination and responsibility, which all faith in a divine government implies; but the philosophical element is always included in the highest forms of religious belief. In this respect, indeed, religion is merely the popular form of metaphysics. Metaphysics and theology, in fact, in their ultimate issue are identical—metaphysics being formally only the more general term for the search into the ultimate ground of all Being, which search, in so far as it does not lose itself in a self-puzzling scepticism, issues necessarily in the assertion of the Eternal Reason, or *Λόγος*, which, in the well-known language of the Apostle John, in the opening words of his Gospel, is only another name for God.

It is a curious fact in the history of the human mind that the most subtle and speculative and scientific people of the ancient world—the Greeks—inherited a religion utterly destitute of this philosophical element, which is so prominent, not only in our Christian religion, but in Brahmanism and other superior forms of popular faith. There is not in the whole breadth of the Homeric poems—and Homer was virtually the Greek Bible—the slightest indication of that great philosophical proposition which stands written on the threshold of the Mosaic Scriptures, "In the beginning God created the heavens and the earth." The old Smyrnean minstrel indicates, indeed, in a familiar line, that the gods of the Jovian dynasty had a father and a mother, whom he distinctly names Ocean and Tethys; * but this fragment of an early theologic speculation—for it is nothing better—bears on the face of it that the existing gods, like the races of men, were born; and any religion in which such gods were supreme could not be said to contain a metaphysics; for every metaphysics must ask not only what is behind the show, but what is before the first. To say that old Ocean and his briny spouse were the father and mother of the gods was nothing more than going another step back in a celestial genealogy of which the origin was in the dark. When you have traced back a pensile chain a thousand links, you are no nearer to a philosophy than when you started, unless you tell us to what the first link is attached. The more current notion among the Greeks was, that the existing dynasty of gods of whom Jove was chief was preceded by two dynasties—the first that of Kronos, whom the Romans identified with Saturn, and the second that of Uranus and Gee, or Heaven and Earth. This implied, no doubt, a philosophical dualism, though in a different style from the dualism of the Good and Evil principle in the religion of the an-

* "Ocean the father of Gods immortal, and Tethys the mother." —Il. xiv. 201.

cient Persians, but still a sort of philosophy. But whether we call this sort of theistic duality a philosophy or not, it is certain that the theory or the fancy was not a living, effective element in the Greek religion. It was a sort of infantile theology, which remained entirely outside of the popular faith and the national worship ; not, as in the creed of all Christian Churches, where a dogmatic theology, or a positive theistic philosophy, constitutes the solid basis and the firm framework of the faith of the Church. Accordingly we find that when the Bœotian poet, Hesiod, who lived some fifty or a hundred years later than Homer, ventured in his capacity of theologer to trace the celestial genealogy a step or two further back, he fell plump into a mighty void, which showed how little there was of deep, thoughtful piety, and how much of superficial impression of the senses and shallow sport of fancy, in what the subtle Greeks had to content themselves with for a theology. Hear how the book of the celestial generations runs. Hexameters are apt to have rather an ungraceful hop in English, but we may try them here for a recreation :—

"In the beginning was Chaos: and afterwards came into being
Earth broad-breasted, the stable upholder of starry Olympus ;

> Darksome Tartarus, too, within the bosom of broad Earth;
> Likewise Eros, the loveliest-born of all the Immortals,
> Thrilling the limbs of men and of gods with gentle emotion,
> Conquering counsel and wit in the charmèd breast of the wisest.
> Erebus, then, and black-stoled Night were children of Chaos;
> Night was mother of Ether, and Day was daughter of Darkness,
> And when Erebus mingled with Night in fruitful embracement,
> Earth then brought into being the might of the starry Welkin
> Like to herself, to spread his vasty curtain around her."

We have nothing here manifestly but a succession of appearances, which no man who meant thinking could mistake for a philosophy of the universe. To call Night the mother of Day, if anything like causal connection be implied, is just as absurd as to say that emptiness is the mother of fulness. When I pour water into an empty tumbler, no doubt the tumbler was empty before it was full; in the order of my sensations the emptiness came before the fulness. That is all. In like manner, when I take my dinner, hunger goes before eating, and is in one sense the cause of my eating; but the cause of there being a dinner to eat is the culinary care of the cook. So, if I build a house, I may say, with Hesiod, In the beginning was the chaos of stones called a quarry, and from that chaos came the beautiful array of curiously co-ordinated stones which I call my house. But everybody sees that without the plan of the thoughtful architect and the skilful hand of the mason, the stones of the quarry could never heap themselves into a house. So it is with all order. To say that as a matter of individual experience in any particular case order proceeded out of disorder, explains nothing; it only states the case to be explained. How did the order come about? This simple question the theology of the Greeks seems never to have even started. Their religion consisted simply in the recognition of an established divine order of things under supreme authority, with reverential submission of the will thereto.

We have now to answer a very natural question: how far is this general consent of humanity a valid argument for theism? If the old sage had any reason for saying *οἱ πολλοὶ κακοὶ, the majority are bad*, might he not have equal or greater ground for asserting the majority are fools? Certainly a mere majority taken by itself would be a very poor argument for the truth of any proposition or for the rectitude of any course of conduct; otherwise all unlimited democracies would always be right, whereas experience has proved that they are peculiarly liable to go wrong. If the majority of persons in any village were given to drunkenness, this certainly would afford no argument in favour of the beauty of intoxication. And, though men often decide very serious matters by mere majorities, is it not rather because they cannot do better than because they have any firm faith that the majorities will be right? If suits on the issue of which many thousands of pounds depend are constantly decided by a majority of judges in the Scottish Court of Session, how often has the decision of that majority been reversed by the decision of a single judge in the English House of Lords? And naturally enough too; for one strong head will always be better than twenty weak heads; and turning the scores into hundreds would only multiply the confusion. And if, looking into the general administration of human affairs in any small town or large city, you should happen to have your eye fastened by any great improvement which has recently been made—such as, for example, the winning of land from the sea, and turning a useless, slimy beach into a beautiful, breezy, green esplanade, as has been done at Rothesay in Bute, or opening up a free prospect and a healthy ventilation—you will find that it was not the majority at all who did or desired these changes, but that some one man of large views and strong will had forced them, in spite of the indifference of the great majority and the violent hostility of a few. In what sense, then, shall we say that the consent of a majority supplies a test, or affords even a presumption of what is right? Plainly not in cases where any very extensive knowledge or subtle views are required; nor in cases where a man can claim no right to have an opinion at all, except after special study, and with professional training; as little in cases where the general judgment has been obscured, and cool discrimination been rendered impossible by the hot smoke and steaming mists of faction, ecclesiastical or civil. Nevertheless there is a preponderant rightness in the sentiment of the multitude, even in their judgments of important public matters, which every one feels in practice, and which even the cool Aristotle defends and illustrates at considerable length in his estimate of the value of democratic forms of government, as opposed to oligarchic.* Perhaps we shall hit the mark here, if we say broadly that, as nature is always right, the general and normal sentiment of the majority must always be right, in so far as it is rooted in the universal and abiding instincts of humanity; and public opinion, as the opinion of

* Pol. III. 11.

the majority, will be right also in all matters which belong to the general conduct of life among all classes, and with respect to which the mind of the majority has been allowed a perfectly free, natural, and healthy exercise. And there will always be a presumption against practices, sentiments, and opinions which run flat in the teeth of universal practice and the unvaried tradition of humanity. It affords a presumption against total abstinence, for instance, as a philosophy of life (for its utility as a special vigorous remedy against a special severe malady may well be admitted), that men of all classes in all ages have been fond of a glass of wine: in like manner it affords a presumption against the Quakers that men of all nations and in all centuries have fought great battles with their neighbours, and become great and strong by the fighting of great battles; and, again, it affords a strong presumption against the notion of dispensing with lawyers, clergymen, physicians, and all professional men—a favourite panacea with some—that in all ages and in all countries such types of the social man have grown up, and found grateful recognition from the majority. And, though the majority of mankind are not philosophers, yet in all matters where nature rules, there is a wisdom in them that justly maintains its ground against the subtle speculations of abstract thinkers who excite attention by confounding things which are naturally distinct, and denying things which the constitution of our nature forces us imperiously to assert. If a glib creature, for instance, calling himself, or being called, a philosopher, should maintain that beauty depends on utility and fitness, you may safely let him spin as many chapters as he may choose in illustration of such a perverse paradox, when everybody knows that the ugliest possible bridge (which the railway companies frequently make) is as useful for its end, and as fit for its purpose, as the most ornamental structure ever devised. The systems of subtle thinkers, in fact, always require to be watched with particular caution : clever people are peculiarly apt to love the fancies of their own begetting, more than the facts of God's creation : though clever, they are not necessarily wise ; and, like Narcissus, will be found sometimes glassing themselves complacently in their own real or imagined perfections, which are very far from exhausting the sum-total of plastic forces in the universe.

CHAPTER II.

REASONABLE GROUND OF THEISM.

"Εστι δή μὲν πρὸς γονεῖς φιλία τέκνοις καὶ ἀνθρώποις πρὸς θεοὺς, ὡς πρὸς ἀγαθὸν καὶ ὑπερέχον· εὖ γὰρ πεποιήκασι τὰ μέγιστα· τοὺ γὰρ εἶναι καὶ τραφῆναι αἴτιοι, καὶ γένομὲνοις τοῦ παιδευθῆναι.

'Ανάγκη εἶναι ἀΐδιον τινὰ οὐσιάν ἀκίνητον. Φαμὲν δὲ τὸν θεὸν εἶναι ζῶον αἴδιον, ἄριστον.

ARISTOTLE.

INGENIOUS novelties of the kind we referred to at the close of last chapter, whether propounded by the logician, or naturalist, by positive philosophers like Plato, or negative philosophers like David Hume, may make men stare for a day, and talk for a century, but they will never stand against Nature. "*Opinionum commenta delet dies, Naturæ judicia confirmat,*" said the great master of old Roman eloquence, and the eloquent expounder of old Roman sense. Build up your Babels of transcendental or paradoxical speculation as high as you please, if they have no root in the fundamental facts of Nature, they are only so much paper; card castles which will fall to the ground easily enough, when the wind changes and the whiff comes. And of these Babels which the perverse ingenuity of men has piled up, there is none against which the verdict of the majority and the loud protest of Nature will more certainly prevail than atheism. Theologians, no doubt sometimes with a shallow impertinence, and a presumptuous dogmatism, may have propounded many things about the character, attributes, and administrative procedure of the Supreme Reason, in protesting against which atheists may justly put in a claim for modesty and wisdom; but when they go beyond this, and instead of the arbitrary dogmas of certain ecclesiastical councils, go to war with the deep-rooted instincts of humanity, they can no more hope to maintain their ground than a little smoke and mist in some muddled locality can obscure permanently the glorious sun in the firmament. For that feeling of reverential dependence of the finite derived reason on the infinite underived reason (the *Λόγος* of John i. 1) is so rooted in all sound reasonable existence that it requires rather a perverse ingenuity to give the opposite thesis—that is all sorts of atheism—the semblance of truth than any peculiar perspicacity to perceive that it is false. If the majority, as Aristotle argues—though there are many fools amongst them, and though they do not a few foolish and mad things occasionally—are nevertheless upon the whole entitled to have a voice in the difficult conduct of public affairs, much more are they entitled, by the primary postulates of all reasonable nature, to protest against such a hollow absurdity as atheism. For the maintenance of the atheistic theory necessarily implies one of three things: either that effects can be produced without a cause; or that a system of reasonable effects can be produced without a reasonable cause; or that the system of effects which we call the world is essentially unreasonable, and therefore does not proceed from a reasonable source. Now of these three atheistic propositions, the negative of the first is of the nature of a postulate to all sane minds; and the wretched cavil about invariable sequence which David Hume introduced, and John Stuart Mill made fashionable for a day, will no more do away with the idea of causality in the great mass of normally constituted minds, than the assertion that the regular going up and down of a piston in a cylinder renders the supposition of a constructive reason in the person of a James Watt superfluous in order to explain the existence of a steam-engine. If physical science can put its fingers on nothing but a series of sequences, it merely proves that science is not philosophy, and is altogether a subordinate affair; but when philosophers, with their most acute spectacles, can see nothing in the world but an infinite series of invariable sequences, the sooner they give up their profession of wisdom the better; for it is just the invariability of the sequences which forces the reasonable mind of man to assert that there is a cause within them, or behind them, which makes the invariability possible. As to the second proposition, that a series of reasonable effects can be produced without a reasonable cause, any sane man—and the more ignorant the better for our present argument—will answer without hesitation, as Cicero did, that when a box of letters, such as are used to teach children the alphabet, shall have tumbled themselves into a well-reasoned treatise, he will believe such proposition, not sooner. The third proposition, the real stronghold of all practical atheism, though at bottom equally untenable, admits of being dressed out in some sentences of plausible pleading, and therefore must be more seriously looked at. The pious theist founds his faith on the wonderful order and beauty, and the exceeding cunning displayed in the architecture of the universe. The most obvious and ready way for the atheist to contravene this argument is to bring into the foreground the contrary of this; and to assert roundly that there is really as much disorder as order in the universe. Of course, for this form of argumentation there are materials at hand of a very formidable look not far to fetch: Neapolitan and Icelandic volcanoes; Lisbon earthquakes; inundations of the Garonne at Toulouse, or of the Dee at Aberdeen; storms, squalls, cyclones, shipwrecks, conflagrations, conspiracies, murders, massacres, idiocies, madness, and all sorts of evil and foolish things which make a prominent figure in the newspapers. But, before we talk on these subjects in a perplexed or, what is worse, in an inculpatory humour, let us consider calmly what our position in this vast universe really is. It is pretty much like the position of a single ant-hill in a vast forest. If you happen to be walking through some pine forest, as at Aviemore or Braemar, with your head very high, and full of fine fancies, let us imagine, you come roughly, with your heel, booted and spurred perhaps, plump into the middle of that metropolis of straws; then what happens? the architecture of laborious weeks is destroyed in a moment, and some scores of those active little intelligences called ants squelched out of existence, at a stroke. Now, suppose one of the ants who had not been squelched, with a particularly sensitive brain, and a great amount of self-importance, being able to make theories like human philosophers, should excogitate a treatise or a tissue of imaginations that might make a treatise to the effect—My beautiful architecture has been destroyed: therefore, either there is no God, or a God who delights in mischief. What think you of this logic? If it is just, then let us all become atheists to-morrow; if it is ridiculous, let us hear nothing more of such nonsense. The real fact is, that in a vast and varied world heaving and swelling, and ramping everywhere, so to speak, with the most eager vitality, collisions and confusions of vital forces will constantly be occurring, which may produce a certain amount of discomfort to individual existences, or even blow them out altogether, but which prove no more the disorder of the universe, than a skit of a boy's squirt can put out the sun. In some parts of the west of Scotland, from the peculiar configuration of the richly varied coast-line, two opposite tides come in, and where they meet make a jabble which disturbs the serenity sometimes of nervous ladies in pleasure-boats. Is there therefore no certain and regular flow in the tides, but only a universal jabble? The whole system of the world, from the wheeling planets in the sky to the little brown ant-hill, or the grey-crusted lichen on the crag, exists in, by, and through a reasoned order: the disorder belongs not to the existence of any one thing, but to points of occasional disturbance arising naturally out of the coexistence of many things. Who can look nakedly on such logic as this, without smiling—"*I have the toothache; therefore there is no God.*" This is the way a clever French writer puts the absurdity of this plea for atheism. It is the product of narrowness of view, and selfishness of feeling. Let Dr. Paley's answer suffice for all such vain talkers:—"The teeth do ache sometimes, but they were manifestly not made for aching."

On the subject of EVIL generally, a great deal of impertinent stuff has been talked—not seldom by very pious people, who forget, in the first place, to tell us what GOOD is; and, in the second place, fail to show us how much of what is good and best in the world could possibly have been produced without the existence of many forms of what is commonly called EVIL. Sir William Hamilton, in one of his chapters, defines pleasure unhindered energy. Very well; this is a sort of pleasure which may suit some persons, or many persons. But there are others—not a few—who will say that they prefer the pleasure which arises, not from the absence, but from the presence, of hindrances. Their notion of happiness is to struggle with difficulties, not to evade them. What, it may well be asked, is the use of energy, if not to struggle with difficulty? But difficulty is only another name for what lazy people call evil; as when virtue is described as an up-hill work, and vice as a prone descent. If virtue were as easy as vice, virtue would cease to be virtue; in other words, in a world where there was no evil there could be no good—at least, no good of the highest kind. If there were no ignorance, how could there be the greedy delight of opening up from ignorance into knowledge? If all men instinctively knew everything, where were the pleasant relation of teacher and taught? If there were no poverty, where were charity? If every person were equally independent and self-reliant, where would be the gracious pleasure on both sides, which arises from the support given by the strong to the weak? Where, again, would be the topping virtue of moral courage, unless the majority, at some particular critical moment, were cowards? Where would be the skill of the pilot, unless there were squalls and unexpected blasts, by which people might possibly be drowned? Where the science of a surgeon, if legs were made of stuff that could not possibly break? And if the garden, left to itself, grew not nettles and thistles and hawkweed and dock, but only roses and potatoes and peas, where were the work of the gardener? In fact, always and everywhere the development of energy implies the existence of that which energy must subdue, namely, evil in some shape or other. Therefore the existence of evil is not a proof that there is no God; but it is by the overcoming of evil constantly that God proves Himself to be God, and man proves himself to be God-like, when, in his subordinate sphere, he does the same. The only real evil in the world is the negative, carping spirit, the Mephistopheles of Goethe's Faust, which, for lack of will to use the given materials in the given way, gratifies an unreasoning restlessness in blaming everything and doing nothing.

These are only a few of the considerations which might be adduced to show how unmeaning are the objections which the atheist brings against the grand and beautiful order of breathing things which we call the world. From our human position and partial point of view the laws of order are not always equally comprehensible; but Disorder is nowhere. If it were to exist at all, the world would very soon cease to be a world; consecutive reason would dissolve into a general babblement of Bedlam; and nothing would remain but a blind weaving and unweaving of a tissue of unintelligent and unintelligible forces. So far is this, however, from being the actual state of things, that the more we penetrate into the hidden workings of Nature, the more we discover that the superficial multiplicity of outward movements is governed by a higher Unity, which pervades and controls all; and this principle is simply God, in whom, as St. Paul says, you and I and all things live and move and have their being. As in a mighty host of hundreds and thousands of men encamped on a battle-field of many miles in extent, movements are constantly taking place which are unintelligible to the private soldier in the position which he occupies, but which all shoot out from the directing mind of the great Napoleon or Moltke of the struggle as clearly and as efficiently as the divergent radiation of the sun; so, most certainly, all the multiplicity of apparently tangled movements in the living machinery of the world, is the manifestation of that self-existent, self-energizing, all-present, all-controlling, all-moulding, reasonable Unity, whom we justly call GOD. Any other theory of the world is either nonentity or nonsense.

CHAPTER III.

ATHEISM; ITS SPECIFIC VARIETIES AND COMMON ROOT.

> "The fool hath said in his heart, there is no God."
>
> PSALMS OF DAVID.

> "Of such doctrine never was there school
> But the heart of the fool,
> And no man therein Doctor but himself."
>
> MILTON.

HAVING in the previous chapter stated, in a few broad lines, the general basis of the theistic creed, I shall now attempt to lay bare the pathology of that most strange disease of the speculative faculty which we call ATHEISM. The history of error is the necessary and most instructive complement of the theory of truth.

And in endeavouring to set forth the causes of this monstrous disease of the reasoning faculty, we shall commence with the simplest conceivable, viz., such absolute feebleness or babyhood of intellect as has not yet reached to the conception of a cause at all. Travellers and anthropological writers tell us of savage tribes whose faculty of discriminating multitude has not reached beyond the number five. Some men, even of well-cultivated minds, but unused to figures, can scarcely perform a simple arithmetical operation without confounding addition and subtraction; and, if so, there may, of course, be creatures so imperfectly emerged from the original monkey-germ of humanity (to speak for a moment with Darwin), and so totally engrossed with putting into some sort of order the multitude of sensuous impressions now being raised into ideas, that the notion of cause has never arisen in their minds. Each individual amongst us remembers a period when curious observation and recognition of individual sensuous impressions formed the sole occupation of budding intellect; and we have only to imagine the growth of the reasoning faculties suddenly stopped in incipient boyhood, in order to realise the notion of a human being incapable of the idea of God. Stunted individuals of all kinds, and stunted races may exist just as trees trying to grow in the Western Hebrides are blasted down to the stature of gooseberry bushes. Atheists, therefore, wherever they may be the natural product of stunted and half-developed intellect, we shall set down in the lowest stage, and call them Atheists of imbecility. But, as we do not go out of our way to see oak trees not bigger than gooseberry bushes, so we need not detain ourselves with this type of intellectual incapables. It is not Atheists of this class that we are likely to meet with in the present age; and if we did meet with them, we should be much more likely to remit them summarily to some hospital of incurables, than to a thinking school where they might be gradually trained up to a comprehension of Leibnitz, and Butler, and Dr. Paley. It is not defect of intellect in ages of civilisation, but perversity, that is the main cause of Atheism.

The next type of the atheistic disease which demands notice has its origin not so much in an intellectual feebleness, as in a moral disorder of the reasonable creature. We may have met sometimes in life, or at all events in the columns of newspapers, with persons of a certain irregular, disorderly, distempered habit of mind with a life and character correspondent. The career of these people is like a piece of music made up of a constant succession of jars which shakes the strings so much by unkindly vibrations, that the instrument, from the force of an unnatural strain, cracks itself into silence prematurely. Now unharmonized characters of this description are naturally indisposed, and practically incapacitated, from recognising order, design, and system in the constitution of the universe; and of course cannot see God. We find, indeed, always in the world only what we bring with us, a capacity of finding. An ass that delights in its own braying, as it is to be presumed all asses do, cannot be expected to find delight in the symphonies of Beethoven; a gambler who has been long accustomed to feed his emotional nature on the irrational stimulus afforded by the blind throw of the dice, loses the capacity of extracting pleasure from the normal exercise of reason; and a drunkard who has destroyed the tone of his stomach by the constant irritation of strong liquors, will turn away from the simplicity of Nature's most healthy beverage as from a poison. It could serve no good purpose to parade in these pages flaming examples of the terrible pranks played by disorderly characters in high places, who showed by their whole conduct that they regarded neither God nor man, but delighted in the production of sheer chaos for the triumph of a grossly selfish energy. The biography of Jack Sheppard may be a very profitable study for young thieves, but honest men will furnish the picture galleries of their brain not with such portraits. Nevertheless, it occurs to me to set down here the features of one of the most notable of those disorderly characters who lived in ancient Rome at that same epoch when the hollow atheism of Epicurus was dressed up for a day in the garb of poetical beauty by a poet of no mean genius called Lucretius. The man I mean is Catiline. Hear how Sallust in a well-known passage describes him: "Lucius Catiline, born of a noble family, a man of great strength, both of mind and body, but of a wicked and perverse disposition. To this man, from his youth upwards, intestine broils, slaughters, rapines, and civil wars were a delight; and in these he put forth all the energy of his youth. He could boast a bodily frame capable of enduring heat and cold, hunger and watching, beyond all belief; he had a spirit daring, cunning, and full of shifts, ready alike to simulate what he was not, and to dissimulate what he was, as occasion might call. Greedy of others' property, he was lavish of his own; in passion fiery; in words copious; in wisdom scant. His unchastened ambition was constantly desiring things immoderate, incredible, and beyond human reach." This is exactly the sort of character, to whose completeness, if anything like a philosophy is to be attributed, atheism will be that thing. For how can the man who delights in turning the social order into chaos cherish the belief that the world is a physical system, moulded and maintained by a spirit of which the essential function is to create order out of confusion, not the contrary? The man, whoever he be, that sets Rome or Paris on fire, is an atheist, and one of the worst type; he not only denies in a speculative way the fair order of the universe, but he actually employs himself systematically in creating disorder. And what does the Roman historian say about the character of the age which produced this sort of monster? Was it remarkable for religion, for piety? Not at all. Hear the words: "When the Romans, who had grown great by labour and righteousness, at length saw all nations subdued, and the world, both sea and land, at their feet, then Fortune began to rage and to confound all things. That very people, who had found it an easy thing to endure any sort of difficulty and danger, found ease and wealth, a blessing to the wise, the source of misery and ruin. First, greed of money, and then lust of power, grew rampant: here was the fuel which fed the flame of all evils. For the greed of money and the haste to be rich sapped the foundations of all faith, probity, and good morals: instead of the old virtues, the desire of wealth taught men insolence, harshness, the neglect of the gods, and general venality; while the love of power forced many men to be false, having one thing in their breast, and another thing on their tongue: friendships were cultivated, not from genuine love, but from some consideration of external advantage; and men were more anxious to show a fair face than to keep a clean breast."

In this striking passage the writer shows us by a terrible example from real life, how true the doctrine of St. Paul is, which, in that awful summation of heathen vice, in the first chapter of the Epistle to the Romans, identifies atheism and immorality as growing out of one common root; not, of course, meaning that all atheists are immoral (for this, as we well know, is contrary to the fact), but that certain epochs of gross social disorder and contempt of all moral restrictions are in their nature always atheistic. "And as they did not like to retain God in their knowledge, God gave them up to a reprobate mind, to do things which are not seemly, being filled with all unrighteousness, wickedness, avariciousness, full of envy, murder, strife, guile, evil habitude, being whisperers, slanderers, haters of God, haughty, insolent, boasters, inventors of evil things, disobedient to parents, senseless, faithless, without natural affection, merciless." For, in fact, the moment the binding power of the great cause of cosmic unity, which we justly call God, is lost sight of, the multitudinous units of human society can no more hold themselves together than the stones of an arch when the key-stone is shaken out. Without this controlling unity to create an organic subordination of part to part, a congregation of human beings naturally resolves into a series of explosions of fitful individualism, which ends in Chaos. That which saves the cosmos at any assignable moment from reeling back into chaos is simply the unity of the self-existent divine reason, controlling the physical world in the first place by what we call laws of nature, and the moral world by what we call the principles of right conduct. Fundamentally both are one ; deny the radical unity of laws of nature in the divine *Λόγος* and you can have no reason to admit a controlling unity of reasonable plan in a well-ordered life, or a well-governed state.

So much for the outstanding extreme types of godless humanity—the atheistic incapable and the atheistic monster. Let us now descend a little into the arena of common modern life, and see what symptoms of the morbid atheistic pathology we may discover there. Now as nettles are seen growing abundantly always where human habitations have been, and every weed has its favourite soil, out of which it seems to spring spontaneously, so all the varieties of speculative and practical atheism which we meet with in common life are weeds sprung from the rank soil of irreverence. As a man cannot eat without an appetite, though all the fruitage of Paradise be spread before him, or as a man with no love in his constitution will see a whole army of Aphrodites marched out without emotion, so neither can gods expect acknowledgment from the sort of creature in whom all reverence for superior excellence is non-existent. Reverence implies a certain inferiority, and certain organs by which the inferior lays hold of the superior, and thereby achieves the pleasant feeling of elevation. But how shall a climbing plant attach itself to the lofty wall, if you cut off its tendrils? So there are human souls that seem to have no tendrils, or whose tendrils have been frosted or nipped off, and thus they remain without any bond of attachment to their natural support. These are the men whom St. Paul, who knew the heathen world well, designates as *ἄθεοι*, or without God in the world (Eph. ii. 12). They drift about in a whirl of unconsecrated passion, or get trampled in the mire, or, what is even more sad, prop themselves up in various absurd ways, boasting that they can do without tendrils, and that only a weakling will cling by the old wall. This want of reverence, which is the natural soil of atheism, may, in some cases, be congenital, like a lack of taste for music, or an incapacity of understanding a mathematical proposition. Some human beings seem shut up in a certain narrow self-containment; to such the recognition of anything beyond their own shell is impossible; for no person expects a lobster to come crawling up to you, and look in your face with the affectionate worship of a dog. Man is, however, naturally not only a weak creature, but a creature who, on only too many occasions, is made sharply to feel his weakness; in his normal state, therefore, he will naturally put forth feelers towards that which is above and beyond him, and that which he seeks to lay hold of for his sustainment, even in the most blind and groping way, he will justly call God. This lowest and simplest form of religion, the mere feeling of dependence on a superior Being, however inadequate, and however far from the sublime of intelligent piety, is nevertheless quite natural; whereas atheism, in a mere piece of ephemeral dependency, such as the strongest man is, must always remain an absurdity and a monstrosity. We shall say, therefore, that man, being naturally a religious animal, atheism can then only spring up when, in the individual or in society, any influence arises which nips the natural bud of reverence in the soul, and perhaps not only deprives this emotion of its healthy nourishment, but furnishes a plenteous supply of fuel to a feeling of isolated self-sustainment. Under this category falls naturally every exercise of strength, power, or force which may inspire the agent with a strong feeling of independence, and incline him, in the pride of the moment, stoutly to disown his dependence on any superior power. Of course in such a creature as man this sort of feeling is mere madness; for the point of a bare bodkin may give a quietus to the earth-shaking bulk of a mammoth as readily as to the minute machinery of a wren. Nevertheless, experience shows amply that this feeling of self-sufficiency, partly natural and partly formed by a favourable circumstance, may grow up to extraordinary dimensions, and teach the petty personality, so intoxicated with his own imagined self-importance, to play a farce of fantastic tricks before high Heaven, which makes men laugh and angels weep. Ancient story, both sacred and profane, is full of instances of this kind; indeed, the wise Greeks, no less than the religious Hebrews, seem to have been possessed with nothing so much as with a sacred fear of the consequences that follow to poor humanity when a just self-esteem grows up into a false self-importance, and a false self-importance is exaggerated into a monstrous self-worship. Hence the frequent repetition of the wise warnings to persons in lofty positions to remember that they are mortal; and the popular image brought before the imperial absoluteness of the Eastern monarch in Herodotus,* or by Horace, in one of his familiar odes, that the lightnings of Jove love to strike the topmost towers. A man is never in greater danger than when, from whatever cause, his spirit, to use the Scripture language,

* History, vii. 10.

is "lifted up," and in the full-blown sense of prosperous power, he forgets how he is girt round with mortal weakness, and conceits himself that he can even cope with the gods. "Is not this great Babylon that I have built for the honour of the kingdom, by the might of my power, and for the honour of my majesty?" says the Chaldean monarch in the Book of Daniel; and we know what happened. A man is never nearer being a beast than when he imagines himself a god. The sentiment which lies at the bottom of all such self-magnification is radically atheistic, essentially monstrous, an inversion of the order of nature—as great as if a man should say that $3-2$ is equal to $3+2$.

> "Demens qui nimbos et non imitabile fulmen,
> Aere et cornipedum pulsu simularat equorum." *

> "Fool, who Jove's thunder and immortal bolt
> Would ape with brass and tramp of hoofèd steeds."

Now of this rebellious strength and insolent usurpation of the throne of the superior by the inferior, the lowest form, of course, is when mere animal strength, planting itself above the intellec-

* Virgil, Æneid, vi. 590.

tual and moral, assumes the reins of government, either in the celestial world or the terrestrial. Of this type of atheism the Giants and others in Greek mythology are a prominent example; the signification of which the reflective Roman lyrist saw clearly. "We know," he says, in one of the most beautiful of those wise and weighty odes which commence the third book—"We know how the impious Titans, the monstrous troop, were hurled into Tartarus by the swooping bolt of Him who alone controls with righteous sway the sluggish land, the windy sea, and the dusky realms of the dead beneath the earth;" for how can it be otherwise, since everywhere in heaven and on earth—

"Vis consili expers mole ruit suâ;
Vim temperatam Di puoque provehunt
In majus: idem odere vires
Omne nefas animo moventes." *

"Strength without counsel falls by its own weight,
But tempered force grows strong and stronger still,
By grace of gods who wisely do abate
The insolent thought and the rebellious will."

And in the same way Homer always characterises his Cyclops, Laestrygons, and other savage and

* Hor. Lib. iii. Carm. iv. 65.

cannibal tribes from whom the ill-starred fellow-sailors of Ulysses find cruel fate as not only inhuman and lawless, but utterly destitute of any notion of religion (οὐδὲ θεουδής, Od. ix.). But it is the intoxication of absolute power in the government of men, more than mere brute strength, that chiefly inclines a mortal man to forget his human limitations and imagine that he can defy the gods, or, what is the same thing, set at nought the eternal constitution of things, by bowing to no superior. "I will take the city, whether Jove wills or wills not!" cried Capaneus, in the pride of assault against the seven-gated Thebes; and the intoxication of self-will, and the madness of self-worship which inspired this famous old sentence, stirs even now the breast of a great Napoleon, dreaming of absorbing vast Europe, or a little Napoleon, scheming in the way of his smaller ambition, for a Rhine boundary. There is an unmistakeable germ of Atheism at the root of all pride.

But it is not only uncontradicted lordship that tends to run into godlessness; unlimited liberty also has its freaks. There is an atheism of democracy, no less than of despotism. Every extreme of self-assertion, or, as the Brahmans would express it, the attempt to make an independent I, whether by violently overriding every other body, or by asserting an absolute independence for each individual, is a rebellion against the firm concatenation of closely subordinated units of which the social framework is composed. From extreme democracy, as from a hotbed, atheism in its rankest stage naturally shoots up. And, accordingly, whether it be in the subtle disputations of ancient glib-tongued Athens, or on the fiery rim of modern French revolutionary craters, or on the more innocent platform of London East-End Sabbath-evening orations, this hideous monstrosity parades itself with observation. How, indeed, should it be otherwise? There is nothing in the idea of mere liberty to create the feeling of reverence; the desire of unlimited liberty is an essentially selfish feeling, and has no regard for any Power from above, that might impose silence on each windy self-proclaimer. The fundamental maxim of all pure democracy is simply this—"I am as good as you, and perhaps a little better; I acknowledge nobody as my master, whether in heaven above or on earth beneath; I will not be fettered." This natural connection between democracy and irreverence it was that caused Plato to make the observation, that even the dogs in Athens had a certain look of impertinence about them which was not observed in Sparta.* And Aristophanes, that large-viewed spectator of the strange and troubled times in which he lived, in his wise burlesque, called *The Clouds*, introduces a democratic and sophist-trained young Hopeful, cunningly arguing himself free from all the restraints of filial duty, and making disobedience to parents one of the household liberties which unfettered democracy was to achieve. Quite consistently too. The insubordinate and rebellious instinct which denies God in heaven, and the king upon the throne, cannot long tolerate the restraints imposed by the natural authority of the father, and the rules of domestic discipline. There is, indeed, no cry more false, more delusive, more contrary to the eternal nature of things, than that which modern democracy has chosen for its favourite watchword—Liberty. No doubt the word has a meaning, and a mighty one, when opposed to all unnatural restrictions of the healthy development of any creature; the instinct of individual self-assertion that makes a slave burst his bonds, or a cap-

* Republic.

tive escape from his prison, will always secure sympathy. But beyond this, in the organization of social life, liberty has very little to do. On the contrary, the whole history of civilisation is a record of successive limitations of liberty, which we call laws. An old Scythian nomad, or modern gipsy, encamped on a Highland moor, and warming himself with the scattered spoils of the old pine forest, is a much more free man than any modern citizen of the most free country in Europe. The civilised man grows, not by a large irregular liberty, but by the wise limitation of his range and the fruitful husbandry of his resources. The first condition of all effective social organization is discipline; but discipline implies subordination; and subordination means the recognition of a supreme authority. Destroy all reverence for such authority, and you produce that feverish, troubled, chaotic state of society which spends its force in continual convulsions and revolutions; while in the individual mind you beget that wanton revelling in the idea of unfèttered individualism which wastes itself in noisy explosions against every power that would tame the fury or prune the rampancy of an imperious *I*.

But unlimited power and unlimited liberty are

not the only social forces that are apt to run riot in the exaggerated assertion of the individual, and the negation of all superhuman authority. There is the irreverence begotten of the pride of intellect. In the exercise of intellectual, as of moral or physical power, there is apt to arise a certain selfish satisfaction in the exclusive dominancy of the knowing faculty above whatever else constitutes the sum of existence in the universe. Knowledge, of course, does not directly produce irreligion, or extinguish piety; on the contrary, the more a wise man knows of the universe, the more is he lost in admiration of its excellence, and in wonder at its mystery; for, as Plato said, wonder is truly a philosophical feeling; and to be full of a living knowledge of things as they are, in their proper relations and proportions, is simply to wonder and to worship. But the knowing faculty is not the whole of a living man, and to bring forth its healthy fruits it must go hand-in-hand with a rich moral nature; divorced from this, that will certainly show itself which St. Paul enunciates: "Knowledge puffeth up, but charity edifieth." In the exercise of the mind's cognitive faculty, isolated from a complete and well-balanced humanity, there is certainly no direct nourishment to the feeling of reverence. Who is more sharp than a lawyer? Who is more clever than a weekly reviewer? Mere knowledge is only one element in the building up of a sound mind. It is not merely that you know, but what you know, and how you know, and how you use your knowledge, that makes your knowledge a power—a legitimate power, let us rather say—otherwise it is a usurpation, and, like all illegitimate powers, smothers that which it ought to protect. Everybody has read Goethe's "Faust." What does that self-vendition of a German soul to the Powers of evil mean? Faust, the speculative sinner, does not go to ruin, like Don Juan, in the Spanish opera, because he flings himself without limitation into the ocean of mere sensual indulgence, putting his private pleasure in the place of God's public order, and thus becoming practically an atheist and a servant of the devil; but he goes to ruin, because he will not accept the bounds of thinking by which all finite being is necessarily confined. He must know everything; all the secret machinery of the universe must lie open to his gaze; the quick lightning of the blood's shooting through the mysterious alleys of vitality, must be measured by his mortal optics; all which simply means, he scorns to be a man with men; he will be a god with gods; he will be his own god. He sets himself above the legitimate authority of that alone self-existent power which creates by limitation; and in doing so, he hands himself over to the destructive Power which, by denying limitation, produces what such denial alone can produce, dissolution and chaos. Thus, in all intellectual, as in all other pride, the root of atheism lies.

But there are various kinds of knowledge; and of all kinds, that which has long had the most evil reputation of begetting atheism is Physical Science. *Tres medici duo athei.* Is this a mere vulgar calumny, or is there any noticeable truth at the bottom of it? Very few such current proverbs are churned out of nothing; and that there is a certain connection between physical science and atheism, the history of philosophy abundantly declares. Democritus of Abdera, the reputed father of the atomistic philosophy, afterwards taught in the Attic gardens of Gargettus with such applause by Epicurus, was the greatest naturalist of his age; and whatever may have been the personal opinions of the laughing sage with regard to the gods, there can be no doubt that the philosophical system expounded by his Attic disciple was utterly godless—worse than godless, indeed; for it is better to deny the gods altogether, than to shunt them off into a cloudy corner of the universe, and give them nothing to do but drink nectar and laugh at limping Vulcan. The explanation of the phenomena of the cosmos, by the various action and interaction of mere force and form which is the sum of the Epicurean doctrine, is pure atheism, and indeed seems to have been meant to put religion out of the world altogether; as we see plainly enough from the tone of the opening verses of Lucretius, in his celebrated Epicurean poem:

> "Tantum religio potuit suadere malorum!"
>
> "Such cruel woes on mortals came from grim religion's power."

And a century before the time of Epicurus we find Aristophanes, in that most intellectual of farces already named, giving the most emphatic prominence to the fact that it was the physical philosophers who, with their talk about atoms and vortices, and collisions and entanglements, and general turmoil in the battle of blind forces, were doing away with the notion of Jove altogether, and substituting happy accident for wise Providence. How far there was a fair apology, or at least a plausible palliative, for the physicists who made broad the phylacteries of this sort of talk long ago, we shall afterwards inquire. For those who revive the doctrine of the construction of a beautifully ordered world by the fortuitous concourse of atoms without mind, nowadays, there is certainly no excuse; but what concerns us specially to state here is, that there is something in the researches of physical science, at least in certain conditions of the intellectual atmosphere, not apparently favourable to the growth of piety and the cultivation of religious reverence. In reading certain of the psalms of David, which must be quite familiar to every English churchgoer, one feels as if walking through a splendid picture-gallery, where not only the pictures are beautiful and grand beyond the power of human description, but, to compensate as it were for the feebleness of the attempt to describe them, the face of the divine artist is made to shine forth constantly behind the frame, and give a living inspiration and an intelligent presence to the scene. But in not a few of our modern physical science books, how different is the feeling! if, indeed, there is any feeling in the matter at all—anything beyond a curious fingering of wretched dumb details utterly destitute of soul. Whatever is in the book, depend upon it God is not there. You will hear no end of talk about laws and forces, developments and evolutions, metamorphic forms, transmuted energies, and what not; but it is all dead—at least all blind. For seeing intellect and shaping reason there is no place in such systems. It is a mere shallow superstition, according to these gentlemen, to imagine any grand design in the system of the Cosmos. There is no construction; there is only a conglomeration, or at best a concatenation. That such Epicurean views are sported nowadays on public platforms admits of no question; that, when philosophically tested, and not allowed to veil their absurdity in a blue mist of fine phrases, they yield nothing but a physical-science variety of atheism, is equally certain; and they naturally provoke us to the inquiry how such unreasoned drivel, after having been exploded for two thousand years, should be revived, and planted on the platform of boastful science as a new revelation which poor benighted humanity should now at length receive with most grateful bewonderment. Of this lamentable upshot of so much high-sounding talk, there are no doubt several causes; but under the present head of our discourse there fall only two to be specially mentioned. First, as before said, because the highest cognitions are never reached by the mere exercise of the knowing faculty, on whatever subject exercised. Instincts and aspirations are higher than knowledge ; and the pretensions of the merely scientific man to assume the dictatorship of things that be are not founded on nature. Many things can be known only by being felt ; all vital forces are fundamentally unknowable ; but they exist not the less because would-be philosopher B or would-be philosopher C has no machinery with which to measure or to control them. Philosophy, itself the most abstract of the sciences, must, as Goethe profoundly remarks, be lived and loved, not merely tabulated and talked about ; and so those who parade mere knowledge as the one thing needful are found at last, as the same Goethe says, counting the parts with their fingers when the spirit has fled. To the meagreness and inadequacy of these knowledge-mongers Wordsworth finely alludes in his description of the various classes of men who might be showing themselves beside the green sod of a poet's grave :—

> " A moralist perchance appears,
>   Led, heaven knows how, to this poor sod :
> And he hath neither eyes nor ears,
>   Himself his world and his own god.

> "One to whose smooth-rubbed soul can cling
> Nor form nor feeling, great or small;
> A reasoning self-sufficing thing,
> An intellectual all in all."

Here the great philosophic poet clearly indicates that without reverence and love, the mere man of science remains incapable of comprehending either humanity or divinity, becomes practically his own god; and is in tone and temper, if not in abstract speculation, an atheist. But it is of the physical science men that we are talking at present; and these also the thoughtful bard of the Lakes shows out from the sacred presence of a true poet of nature, with a sharp tone of quiet contempt, as follows:—

> "Physician art thou? one all eyes?
> Philosopher? a fingering slave,
> One that could peep and botanize
> Upon his mother's grave!"

Of course general charges against whole classes of men are not for a moment to be understood here; but the writer takes a strongly-marked man of the type, and this, like "the girl of the period," serves the purpose, though a man may live largely in the period without perhaps meeting him or her more than once. But the physicist, by the very nature of his occupations, is unfavourably situated in regard to the knowledge of spiritual things. He is all eyes and all fingers; and confessedly neither with the fleshly eye can one see God, nor with the fleshly finger can one handle Him. And so it comes about that a physicist, when left to the meagre resources of his own science of externalities, may come not to believe in mind at all, and of course to deny God. Let him torture nature as he will, strike out all sorts of flashing electricities, pry curiously into the secret spring-work of vital machinery by monstrous vivisections, yet he cannot lay his finger on God. There is therefore no God—nothing that he can lay his finger on; therefore nothing at all; only talk about laws and forces, and an eternal blind struggle of the stronger to kick the weaker out of the room. Such is the sad fashion by which the study of mere physical science, unelevated by a high religious philosophy, runs into the blank vacuities and blind fortuities of atheism. It must always be so. No pyramid ever stood upon its apex, and no reasonable explanation of a reasonable world can be evolved from a tabulation of mere externalities. The kingdom of true knowledge, like the kingdom of heaven, is within. No philosophy worth the name was ever arrived at by external induction. By induction dead shells may be gathered, but the life of the soft-bodied creature which inhabits the shell is produced by the living power of Divine Reason, the soul of this mysteriously-ordered world, which eludes all microscopes to behold, and defies all pincers to grasp.

I have spoken hitherto mainly about the men of physical science, because since Bacon, they have been making large their phylacteries in this country, and stirring the minds of men wonderfully. There are reasons for this ; and for the brilliant antediluvian, pre-Adamitic and other discoveries which they have made, we may feel disposed kindly to forgive them a little nonsense. A wise man on a hobby-horse is never an edifying spectacle ; but the creature delights himself for a lifetime perhaps, and we are amused for an hour. Let us now look in another direction. There is no nonsense like learned nonsense ; and of all learned nonsense, metaphysical nonsense is the most extravagant. Of course among other forms of insane abstract speculation, we have metaphysical atheism ; and the father of this sort of nonsense, in modern times, was a Scotsman, David Hume.

No man, I presume, who has read his works will deny that Hume was a very clever fellow, a very agreeable, gentlemanly fellow too, and a man who combined a knowledge of books with a knowledge of men to an extent very rarely exhibited in the country which produced him; still he talked nonsense about causation, and about the ultimate cause; and this nonsense is to be traced in the case of the metaphysician, as in that of the physicist, ultimately to a want of reverence in his character, aided by a certain flatness, and shallowness, and want of earnestness in the age to which he belonged. With regard to metaphysical nonsense generally, and the atheism which it will occasionally produce, we must bear in mind what Professor Ferrier says, in the first chapters of his profound work on Consciousness. Of all men, says that subtle and substantial thinker, the metaphysician is most apt to run himself into the blind alley of some inextricable absurdity; for he aims at explaining the very complex machinery of the vasty universe by some one favourite principle, or method; and, if this principle be either wrong in itself, or wrongly applied, or if it contains only one half the truth, or only a certain attitude and aspect of the truth, the whole of the ingeniously spun system becomes a gossamer web, not strong enough to hold a fly. What Hume said, for instance, about the comparison of a piece of human architecture, with the architecture of the universe, that we know everything about the one, and can know nothing about the other, is true only in so far as organized growth is a much more excellent and a much more divine thing than the best compacted masonry; manufactures of all kinds we can produce; growth of any kind, from the branching foliage of tropical vegetation to the tiniest spot of grey lichen on a bare rock, defies the most cunning of our scientific appliances. Here no doubt is a gap; but on the other hand, the grand congruities of eternal Reason shine out as plainly in the divine architecture as in the human; and the intellectual process of the universe, which we call growth, is not the less intelligible because it is not merely mechanical, but only the more wonderful. Another of the pretty sophisms, with which the Scottish sceptic, as we remarked in the last chapter, strangled his healthy human instinct, was that about causation. Of course what many superficial observers call a cause, is only a point in an invariable sequence; it needed no philosopher to tell us this; but when he, and a whole school of meagre puzzlers after him, told us seriously that causation means only invariable sequence, we are inclined to subscribe to any nonsense in the Council of Trent, and to any horrors in the most damnatory creed, rather than fill our bellies with such East wind, and believe it to contain any virtue that makes warm blood. There is not a sane man out of Bedlam who will not confess, when the thing is properly put before him, that the invariability of any sequence is just the very thing that renders the idea of a cause necessary: as necessary in fact to the constitution of a reasoned universe, as some fundamental axiom is to the proof of a mathematical theorem. But your metaphysician will not see this; he must have a special transcendental region for himself, where he may make unhindered all sorts of abstract postures and somersets and curious antic wriggling, at which He who sitteth in heaven shall laugh; and so rather than believe a creative mind with Moses, or a plastic reason with Plato, he sets himself in a pretentious wordy way to evolve all things out of a dark hollow centre of nothingness, and bind them together with a girdle of black impenetrable necessity. Surely wise men, who talk such things, have been taken in the net of their own subtleties, while out of the mouths of babes and sucklings, in modern as in ancient times, God hath perfected praise.

It is always more safe, in matters of healthy human sentiment, to trust to poets than to philosophers. A living sympathy with nature never can lead you far wrong. Men of the calibre of Homer, Shakespeare, Robert Burns, and Walter Scott, never strangle the broad realities of nature with ingenious and unsubstantial subtleties. A poet is naturally a religious animal; we shall not, therefore, presumably expect atheism from him; nevertheless, we had Lucretius; and some of our most brilliant notorieties in the modern world of song, are not the most notable for piety. Let us inquire, therefore, lastly, by what extravagant and erring flight the bright-winged creature called a poet may sometimes be charmed away into the dim limbos and dark vortices of a godless cosmos. Other causes of such blind plunges will be noticed afterwards; the present order of our discourse only calls on us to remark, that there may be an idolatry of the imaginative, as well as of the knowing faculty. Reverence no doubt is as necessary to the complete poet as love; but just as a man may have a grand swing of the imaginative faculty, and yet be wayward, wilful, and extremely selfish—like Lord Byron—so it is possible for a rhymer to have in his brain-chamber a perfect kaleidoscope of shifting beauties, and yet lack that veneration for the grand central truth of the universe which gives elevation to all beauty, and significance to all variety. The Greeks had one very valuable idea, that a poet was always a *σοφός*, a wise man, and the best definition of poetry, to suit their practice, would be harmonious wisdom. But in our age of multiplied specialties, we are too apt to run after dexterity in artistical exhibition, without regard to health of tone, sanity of meaning, or naturalness of expression. Poetry, of course, as well as music and dancing, may luxuriate amply in this direction ; and the sacred art of the poet, of which the virtue is by truthful and vivid pictures to teach the wisdom of life, and justify the ways of God to man, may degenerate into a succession of dexterous pyrotechnic displays, and startling explosions of brilliant egotism, in which no worship dwells. Thus a practical divorce between poetry and piety may take place ; and though no direct war be proclaimed against religion—as in Lucretius—a pious man feels a sort of want in the effusions of poets of this defective type, somewhat as if one were to walk through

Windsor Palace, and see splendid traces of everything but the Queen. Let the young poet, therefore, beware of glorying too much in his strength. A man may do anything, said the wise old octogenarian of Weimar, except live at random, *sich gehen lassen.* Floating about on rosy clouds for mere self-delectation, or flashing forth a series of iridescent coruscations for the amusement of those who seek for excitement, rather than improvement, will never exhaust the function of "the pious bards who speak things worthy of Phœbus." To attain this dignity there must be a consecration of the whole man, his natural genius, and his acquired dexterities, to the service of the great Architect, in whose living temple the highest honour the best of us can achieve is to be serviceable stones.

Thus much for atheism, speculative or practical, declared and marked, or only insinuated and indicated, when viewed as proceeding from the want of a root of reverence in the soul. In the next two chapters I shall consider the phenomena of this abnormal state of mind, where it seems to spring rather from an exaggeration, or misdirection, than from a deficiency of the noble emotion of wonder; and I shall then conclude with considering how far atheism, or at least an absence of natural piety, may in many cases be only the rebound of an ill-balanced mind from the asperities and the rigidities of some local orthodoxy. If there is rebellion anywhere in a State, the Government is seldom altogether free from blame.

CHAPTER IV.

POLYTHEISM.

"Fragilis et laboriosa mortalitas in partes ista digessit, infirmitatis suæ memor, ut portionibus coleret quisque quo maxime indigeret."—PLINY.

POLYTHEISM is not atheism certainly on the very face of the word; many gods can never mean no god; and therefore the intelligent reader may justly ask what is it doing here? The answer is simply this, that we have to do in this discourse not merely with abstract beliefs, but with practical consequences which flow from them; not with the abstract denial of a God, but with the concrete existence of such fancies, notions, or dogmas about God, as practically result in a denial of a divine order and beauty and harmony in that reasoned unity of things which we call the world. When in a well-known passage of his epistle to the Ephesians (ii. 12) St. Paul talks of the members of the

Christian Church in that part of the East as having lived formerly the slaves of all sorts of base lusts and passions without God—*ἄθεοι*—and without hope in the world—though the word *ἄθεος* is no doubt frequently used by classical writers to signify a man holding dogmatically what we call atheistical opinions—there is no reason to suppose that he had any such shallow dogmatists specially in view; but a man with him is an atheist, even though perhaps paying worship to some gods, or demons—like the Ceylonese—who as a matter of moral fact shows by all his conduct that he believes in no established order of a great social brotherhood of men born of a common father, but recognises only his personal will, and special passion as the legitimate motive power of human conduct. Or, to take a simile from political life, that man is a traitor and a rebel not only who pastes a public proclamation up in the market-place that the king has no right to reign, but much more rather the man who refuses to pay the taxes, disdains the accepted tokens of homage, and draws his sword for the head of his own clan, and in the cause of his own kinship only, not for the head of the State. So, if the celebrated Macdonald of the Isles lost his haughty position in the Hebridean seas, was fined of his lordship, and swept all his clan with himself into ruin as the natural issue of his reiterated attempts to shake off the legitimate authority of the monarch to whom he had sworn fealty, in the same way it may be in the religious world, that if any people prostrate themselves before gods which are no gods, and whose intervention hinders the true God from being seen and recognised, they may be guilty of a conduct which is practically as bad, or even worse, than absolute atheism. For religious atheism—that is, atheistical doctrine—means only an absence of all positive theological contents, and may be quite consistent, as in the case of Buddha to be presently considered, with a strict observance of the great moral laws that bind society together, and even with a belief in the necessary moral consequences of actions, entailed from generation to generation—as, indeed, the Buddhists believe of all men most firmly ; but the misdirected reverence and utterly unreasonable religiosity of some forms of superstition, may in its effect on social life amount to what the mathematicians call a minus quantity, that is, something worse than nothing ; as certain kinds of food, though not immediately poisonous, may by the presence of some element unfavourable to a healthy vitality, lead by sure degrees to the disruption of the system. This consideration it was which led Plutarch and other wise ancients to discuss the question *whether atheism or superstition is the more pernicious?*—a question which manifestly admits of no clear answer; for, while on the one hand there may be an intellectual atheism associated with so much practical goodness as to make it socially innocuous, there may, on the other hand, be a moral atheism ramping so wildly through all the organism of society, and disturbing the machinery of human life to such a degree as to render many kinds of degrading superstition less dangerous. Our inquiry, therefore, into the origin and character of polytheism, as connected with atheism, will tend to bring into view two important aspects of that misdirected reverence, too often confounded; first, that aspect of polytheism in which the good so predominates as to make it in a social point of view emphatically preferable to all forms of atheism; and secondly, that more degraded aspect which presents itself when neither poetical grace, nor gracious moral influences, nor an underlying consciousness of dimly-shadowed monotheism, contributes anything to redeem the absurdity, or mitigate the baseness of a reverence fathered by fear, and a worship inspired by selfishness. And in setting forth the most obvious propositions belonging to this interesting theme, if we confine ourselves mainly to illustrations from the Greek religion, it will be because we shall thus be using materials with which all educated persons in this country are to a certain extent familiar, and in the right theological use of which they will naturally feel an interest.

On the origin and significance of the mythological theology of the Greeks and other polytheistic races, no small amount of nonsense, both learned and unlearned, will be found loading the library-shelves; and this is not at all to be wondered at, considering that the most original and imaginative thinkers on the subject often want the requisite learning; while men of learning too frequently are destitute not only of that fine feeling for the poetry and piety of nature which belongs specially to all mythological interpretation, but of the sound common sense and freedom from favourite fancies which is necessary to the recognition of truth in any quarter. But after the full and thorough discussion which Greek mythology has received during the present century, specially from the Germans, and the wider range of induction opened up to scholars by the Oriental excursions of the Sanscritists and other comparative philologers, we have no difficulty now in planting our foot on at least one broad basis of scientific certainty in this field. Favourite theories and darling speculations of various kinds being blown away, a sound eye can discern clearly the great physical forces of nature as lying at the root of the luxuriant growth of motley and grotesque, or graceful, beautiful, and sublime figures which composed the popular Pantheons of India and Greece. Not that other elements sometimes did not enter into the composition of this popular theology; but in the main the forces of external nature, figured by imagination and fired by passion, formed a groundwork of all polytheistic idolatry, at once the most natural and the most extensive. Let us endeavour to realise to ourselves how this took place. Let us drop out in imagination the knowledge of the one true God from the centre of our fundamental ideas with regard to the Universe—of which ideas the unity of the Divine nature in all Christian countries forms now the keystone—and see what remains. Imagine a creature such as man in the first stages of society historically was—of quick sensibility, vivid imagination, hasty passion, overpowering emotion, limited knowledge, and small speculation—sometimes, no doubt, grandly conscious of his own power as a living being of great energy and scope, but not rarely possessed, or it may be oppressed, by the feeling of his own feebleness, helplessness, and dependence. Dependence on what? Place yourself in thought in the middle of a broad dreary moor during a thunderstorm, or on the surge of a foaming sea fretted with reefs, in a ship without a pilot, or at the bottom of a smoking mountain, spouting sulphurous clouds, and pouring forth rivers of red molten rock over the works and ways of mortal men, and you will feel in a moment that your life is continually at the mercy of three elements—AIR, WATER, and FIRE, before whose manifestations of might and violence, the strongest mortal is as weak as a straw in the whirlwind, or a worm beneath the tramp of a rhinoceros. What then will a poor, ignorant, helpless creature, without special light, in these circumstances naturally do? He will cry out and appeal to the element, or the force behind the element—let it be AIR, WATER, or FIRE—with which he has for the moment to do; and this element, in defect of further generalisation, will become a god; not the material element, however, simply as we are apt to conceive it in modern language, or a form of what we call matter, but the energetic totality of the thing exercising a power, apparently of a similar nature to that which we exercise when we put forth our arm, and produce similar effects. The Air, therefore, or the Fire, or the Water, is conceived dimly as a person, at least as exercising the functions of a person; it is a superhuman, incalculable, transcendental force—that is, comparatively a divine power, and therefore will naturally, if curious reason does not interfere, be recognised and, by some sort of homage or worship, acknowledged as a god. And this hasty generalisation, as the logicians would say, will have at least one striking fact in its favour, of which it will require some considerable advance in science, some ripeness in speculation, or some special revelation to rebut the force. These potent elements, of which feeble man seems as it were the sport, do not by any means to the vulgar eye present the aspect of harmonious and concentuous powers; they rather stand forward in the attitude of antagonists, to struggle and to battle together, to overwhelm, overmaster, neutralise and annihilate one another in a most unfriendly way. We are therefore, at our first encounter with one of these outbursts of apparently unreined and unruly power, at a very far remove from the idea of the Divine UNITY. Thus we have got, by a single step, at the constitution of a separate divine force for Air, Water, and Fire, which, by-and-by, the natural action of a vivid imagination will shape into the complete figure of a thundering Jupiter, an earth-shaking Neptune, and a metal-melting Vulcan, with all the appropriate badges, weapons, and appurtenances, that with chastened taste in the West and grotesque symbolism in the East would naturally attach themselves to such personages.

Let us now look to the evidence from historical and literary fact. We had occasion to mention already, in our first paper, that Homer distinctly mentions OCEAN as the great progenitor of the Hellenic gods; and, though this god was rather an antiquated personage in the days of the poet, and comes up more as a sort of fossil witness or an underlying stratum of old popular tradition, the famous verse (Il. xii. v. 245) in which his name occurs is only the more significant as a stereotyped proof of the original element out of which the fully equipped equestrian Poseidon afterwards started into being. But even in later days the same undisguised element plays its part with the other most ancient gods in the well-known tragedy of Æschylus, from which Shelley, Byron, Goethe and others have drawn such favourite inspiration.* In the same way, we find that, though the golden-locked Apollo, the celestial archer, has in familiar Greek theology completely displaced the original sun out of which he grew, nevertheless, this undisguised elemental sun, this bright, all-seeing, all-commanding Helios — ἥλιος — keeps his ground, distinctly acknowledged in the most solemn form of oath which a pious Greek could take into his mouth.

> Father Jove, from Ida swaying God most glorious and great,
> And thou, Sun, the all-pervading and all-hearing power, and ye
> Rivers and Earth.†

And so with the rest. To an eye once open to the fact that the great embodied celestial and terrestrial forces, which form partly the stage and partly the atmosphere of our human life, were the original gods of Greece, it requires no accidental or extended recognition by the Greek poets to enable it to see through the thin veil of human personality under

* The "Prometheus Bound," in the introductory scenes.
† Iliad, iii. 277.

which their elemental significance lay concealed. Plato, and thinkers much below his range, saw the truth and spoke it out plainly ; * and, in fact, a mere modern poet, from the reverential contemplation of the varying forms and forces of Nature, will often reconstitute the persons of the Greek Pantheon without any formal historical tradition ; and a man must be dull indeed who does not see in all the epithets of Jupiter and Neptune, the most obvious impersonations of the thunderous atmosphere and the billowy main. A dark-browed king, girdled with dark-blue clouds, driving across the copper-floor of the firmament, in a chariot of thundering steeds, with a flashing bolt in his hand, and an eagle in ministering attendance, this is exactly the figure that a poetical imagination would body forth, when wishing to give a human shape to the awful Divine Force which lies in that perturbation of the aerial elements which we call thunder. And, if ships are called in poetical language " the white-winged coursers of the deep," how is it possible for a poetical mind, embodying in human form the divine

* " It seems plain that the original inhabitants of Greece worshipped the same gods as are now acknowledged by the majority of the Barbarians, as the Sun, the Moon, the Earth, the Stars and the Sky."—Cratylus, p. 397. D.

form of the foaming billows, to avoid the image of a long-bearded charioteer, crowned with chaplets of seaweed, and bounding from wave to wave in a chariot drawn by cerulean steeds, with troops of gods, half-man, half-fish, blowing shells behind? All this lies upon the surface, and calls for no erudite research or curious commentary. But let us take a familiar instance a little less obvious to the unprofessional eye, but not less certain to a well-schooled mythologer. What were the HARPIES? Not a few of our readers will remember, from their school-days, how the "pious Æneas," in the course of his long sea-wanderings and stormy toils to found the mighty Rome, after leaving Crete and rounding Cape Matapan, landed upon certain rocky islands to the west of Greece in the Archipelago called the Strophades, and there, with his wearied crew, sat down on the beach to take some needful refreshment; but scarcely had they sat down—

> When lo! the Harpies with horrific swoop
> Leap from the hills, and fearful-clanging wings
> And with their obscene claws invade the feast
> And spread pollution o'er the board, with blasts
> Pestiferous, and screams, that rend the ear.*

* Æneid iii. 225.

At this unseemly interruption from their prepared meal, the voyagers rise in wrath, seize their swords, and commence a vigorous offensive war against their rude assaulters. But in vain. Like Macbeth's witches, they fly off, receiving no scaith from touch of mortal blade ; and, perched on the top of an adjacent cliff, the leader of the filthy chorus, called Celæno, screeches forth a hideous prophecy against the much-enduring founders of imperial Rome. In mythology, as indeed in the early history of all original races, names are always significant ; but the name of this personage, Celæno, meaning in Greek BLACK, will not help us far in the interpretation of the myth. When we turn to Homer and Hesiod, however, the names of these vaporous Seizers (so Harpies means, from ἁρπάζω) publish their elemental significance in terms too plain for commentary. Hesiod, the earliest doctor of theology, and acknowledged theologer of the Greeks, in his genealogy of the gods gives the following account of the pedigree of the Harpies :—

Thaumas married Electra, the daughter of deep-flowing Ocean :
She to Iris gave birth, the swift, and she to the Harpies,
Beautiful haired, AELLO yclept, and OCYPETE, maidens
Swiftly-winged to follow the path of the bird, or the vagrant
Breeze on the brae.

Now these two names signify, the one *whirlwind*, and the other *swift-swooping;* so that their names alone declare their nature, as plainly as the moral characters of the various pilgrims are expressed by their names in Bunyan's popular allegory; and though it rather appears that in the case of Apollo Homer and his brother-minstrels had no notion of his original identity with the elemental Helios or the Sun, yet in the case of the Harpies the poet plainly indicates his consciousness of their original character, when he says of the daughters of Pandarus in one line that they were snatched away by the Harpies, and in another line that they were snatched away by the whirlwinds.* We have here, therefore, a plain case of mythological personages, playing a sort of equivocal part between the element of which they were the impersonation, and the anthropomorphic impersonation itself. In the hymns of the Rig-Veda—thanks to the labours of Max Müller, and other learned Sanscritists—this sort of equivocal, half elemental, half anthropomorphic divine powers may be seen in great numbers, and studied to great advantage.

We have placed this case of the Harpies in some detail before the reader till he may be able to judge

* Odyssey, xx. 66 and 77.

for himself, from what root of scholarly induction the true meaning of mythological personage may be evolved. How the direct intuition of a poetic mind familiar with the striking aspects and the vital significance of natural scenery, may, without learned research, flash forth the deepest significance of these matters in the most graceful way, the following passage from Wordsworth will most effectively declare—

> "Once more to distant ages of the world
> Let us revert, and place before our thoughts
> The face which rural solitude might wear
> To the unenlightened swains of Pagan Greece.
> In that fair clime, the lonely herdsman, stretch'd
> On the soft grass, through half a summer's day,
> With music lulled his indolent repose;
> And, in some fit of weariness, if he,
> When his own breath was silent, chanced to hear
> A distant strain, far sweeter than the sound
> Which his poor skill could make, his fancy fetched,
> Even from the blazing chariot of the Sun,
> A beardless youth, who touched a golden lute,
> And filled the illumined groves with ravishment.
> The nightly hunter, lifting a bright eye
> Up towards the crescent-moon, with grateful heart
> Called on the lovely wanderer who bestowed
> That timely light, to share his joyous sport:
> And hence, a beaming goddess with her nymphs,
> Across the lawn and through the darksome grove,
> Not unaccompanied with tuneful notes
> By echo multiplied from rock or cave,
> Swept in the storm of chase: as moon and stars

> Glance rapidly along the clouded heaven,
> When winds are blowing strong. The traveller slaked
> His thirst from rill or gushing fount, and thanked
> The Naiad. Sunbeams upon distant hills
> Gliding apace, with shadows in their train,
> Might, with small help from fancy, be transformed
> Into fleet Oreads sporting visibly.
> The Zephyrs fanning, as they passed, their wings,
> Lacked not, for love, fair objects whom they wooed,
> With gentle whisper. Withered boughs grotesque,
> Stripped of their leaves and twigs by hoary age,
> From depth of shaggy covert peeping forth
> In the low vale, or on steep mountain side;
> And, sometimes, intermixed with stirring horns
> Of the live deer, or goat's depending beard,
> These were the lurking Satyrs, a wild brood
> Of gamesome Deities: or Pan himself,
> The simple shepherd's awe-inspiring God."

The genesis of mythological theology from the action of a reverential imagination on the forms and forces of external nature, being thus explained in a few prominent instances, we have next to bear in mind that the tendency to elevate such imaginative pictures into personal gods, and clothe them with human attributes, having once set in, could not be expected in the general case to confine itself to the few striking instances from which it started. It was possible, indeed, to have made the start from the moral physical dualism of HEAVEN and EARTH, as in Hesiod; or from the moral dualism of the Good and Evil principle, as in the theology of the ancient Persians, and to stop there; but the moment that a separate God has been assigned to the thunder, and another to the Sun, the creation of an uncounted multitude of separate divine personalities was as natural and necessary as the growth of a broad-branching tree from a small seed. Division and subdivision, as so beautifully described in Goethe's poem of the Metamorphosis of Plants, is the law of growth in Nature, and the law of development in imaginative theology. Now observe what follows. Not only the grand and overwhelming, but at the same time comparatively definite and well-marked forces of external nature, but the more mysterious and incalculable, and often strongly unmanageable emotions and passions of the inward man, come in for their full share of individualized deification; and these passions and emotions, being recognised only as divine Forces, will naturally receive their allotment of worship without any attempted distinction between the moral good and evil from which they spring, or the good and evil consequences to which they tend. Altars will be erected to FEAR* and to FEVER, as well as to

* "*Tullus in re trepidâ aras* PALLORI *et* FAVÒRI *vovit.*"—Livy i. 27.

JUSTICE and to MERCY. And not only so, but if we take, for instance, the worship of impersonated passions, in themselves natural, healthy, and good, such as the worship of vital enjoyment, under the form of DIONYSUS, the planter of the vine, and of sexual sympathy, under the form of Aphrodite, it is easy to see that fervent devotion to such divine forces might easily degenerate into hot-beds of the most vulgar sensualism. Generally, indeed, we may see in Polytheism, as we have sketched its origin, a radical vice in the want of a definite and well-marked line between moral right and wrong in the objects of popular worship, so that even at its best, that is when, as in Greece, it was inspired and moulded by a pervading spirit of beauty, it makes its appeal to the æsthetical rather than to the moral faculties of our compound nature: being, also, as we have seen in its origin, without any regulating power, it is free on all sides to run into rampant excess; in which case the application of the proverb will not be far to seek, *corruptio optimi pessima*—the corruption of the best is the worst. When good things are bad, they are very bad. Let us see, then, by an example, how these things acted in practice among our model-polytheists, the ancient Greeks.

In the minute topographical description of Athens given by the antiquarian traveller of the second century—Pausanias, the Grose of Greece—we find the following passage:—"In the market-place (*ἀγορά*) of Athens, among other remarkable things not generally noticed, is an altar of MERCY, a goddess, to whom, on account of her manifest utility in all the changes of human life, the Athenians, but the Athenians alone, pay reasonable worship. For this people, of all the Greeks, are not only the most humane and civilized in all social matters, but they are specially notable for their piety; * and besides this to MERCY, they have erected altars to REVERENCE, and to RUMOUR, and to IMPULSE. And we see from this plainly how those states which are most distinguished for piety, are at the same time most favoured by the gods in the matter of prosperity and good fortune." And to show how this worship of MERCY and REVERENCE acted in practice we have only to appeal to a well-known passage in the Oedipus Coloneus of Sophocles, in which the

* The Bible reader will recall the introductory words of St. Paul's famous Address (Acts xvii.), though these commentators are certainly wrong who suppose that the word δεισιδαιμονέστερος in this passage is used in a complimentary sense by the apostolic writer.

penitent son of the injured old monarch, using the strongest appeal to move the heart of his wrathful parent, says:—

> "For MERCY sits with Jove upon the throne
> In every doom: so may she not from thee
> Sit far, my father!"

But an example from historical fact will perhaps be better. The elegant Greek humourist, Lucian, in that charming morsel of biography entitled "Demonax," relates that this philosopher, who had a remarkable power over the Athenians, on one occasion, when the citizens, from a rivalry with the Corinthians, were proposing to get up an exhibition of gladiators after the manner of their then masters, the Romans, stood up publicly and said—"Do not, men of Athens, bring forward a bill for any such purpose, till you have rooted away the altar of Mercy so prominent in your market-place." In such cases it is plain that, however founded in an intellectual error and in one sense atheistical, as worshipping the creature rather than the Creator, Polytheism was calculated to exercise, and actually did exercise, a moral power of singular effectiveness. In fact, as we see every day, a mere orthodoxy of the head in the

Christian world, without any such practical issues as this intellectual rightness is calculated to produce, so, on the other hand, gross intellectual error may exist along with remarkable moral rightness. The question, therefore, whether in any particular religion Polytheism may not be more dishonouring to God than Atheism, depends partly on the nature of the deities worshipped, partly on the capacity of the people worshipping for making the best use of slippery and equivocal materials; partly, also, on the counterbalancing forces which any Polytheistic form may contain within itself, neutralising the consistent action of its own worst elements. With these tests in our hand, we can have little difficulty in perceiving that, though Greek popular theology contained certain elements whose ignoble issues completely justified the condemnation passed upon it by St. Paul in the first chapter of the Romans, it was in the main, at least in its palmy days, morally beneficent in its tendency, and as such, we may say less dishonouring to God, and less monstrous in man, than even the most moral forms of cold, self-contained, unsympathetic, and essentially unhuman Atheism. It was impossible, indeed, that a people so nobly endowed as the Greeks, and whose genius had elevated the rude songs of an annual harvest-home into such a lofty platform of moral teaching as we find in the tragedies of Æschylus, Sophocles, and Euripides,* should have failed to let the grosser elements of their physical theology drop, and to bring into the foreground what higher elements in that group of motley forces were calculated to stir the noblest chords in the human heart, and elevate their worshippers to some likeness of the more perfect beings whom they believed. And, accordingly, we find that the favourite patron-goddess of the Athenians, whose far-glittering spear the sea-tossed sailor greeted as he rounded the Sunian promontory, was in point of moral character as elevating an object of worship as any purest saint in the Christian calendar. No doubt, this same Pallas, in the "Iliad,"† teaches Pandarus to break a truce sealed by the most solemn oaths. But this glaring violation of one of the most weighty points of the moral law, in the person of the flashing-eyed daughter of the supreme ruler of Olympus, is one of those inconsistencies which are

* "The preaching power, as we may call it, of the Greek stage as a pulpit, will be best realised by reading the Furies of Æschylus, and the opening chorus of the Agamemnon by the same lofty genius."

† Book iv.

readily condoned to the patriotic partiality of the poem, and the unsuspecting simplicity of the poet. We must bear in mind, also, that no people, though it carries along with it the forms of expression belonging to the crude theology of an early age, is practically influenced, in its stages of higher social growth, by all that such crude forms of expression would consistently seem to imply. On the contrary, a certain inconsistency is the salvation of all popular creeds; and Plato must perhaps be looked on as somewhat pedantic, or, at least, as over-severe, when in the second book of his ideal polity he inveighs so seriously against the theological teaching of the great national minstrel. Homer, no doubt—the poet, as they called him—had an immense moral influence over every Greek mind; but his poems were secular, not sacred; and no person was obliged to make a formal subscription to all his theological teachings, as if they were divine oracles. On the contrary, the wise Greeks reserved to themselves the complete right of excluding from their articles of faith any fact or fable asserted of the gods which they considered as unworthy of the Divine Nature. In Aristophanes it is quite true that a disobedient son is introduced who justifies his insolence to his father by the treatment which Father Kronos receives from young Jove, in the mythological allegories. But the Greeks had sense enough to know that things said or done about the gods in the comic department of their religious exhibitions—for the drama was part of the national religion—were said or done only to excite a laugh, and could be said and done, as they were said and done, only because everybody knew that no reasonable man would think of transferring such jokes to the sober guidance of life, when holiday fun was over. Had such jokes been perpetrated on the serious stage of tragedy, nay, had even any impropriety been committed in the dignified dress and costume of the gods, we have the best authority for saying that the religious feelings of the public would have been grossly outraged, and the author would have been censured by the authorities.* But the great salt of the Greek mythology, and which kept it, even in its worst days, from sinking into a state of putridity and pollution more degrading than many forms of atheism, which it was perfectly capable of when this antidote ceased to act, was the central truth of the supremacy of Jove as the moral ruler of the universe—a supremacy, in fact, which con-

* See Lucian, Piscator, ch. 33.

stituted a sort of MONOTHEISM working powerfully behind scenes, and saving Polytheism from that sensualistic anarchy into which, without such steerage, it would inevitably have been plunged. On this characteristic of Greek Polytheism, too often lost sight of, or not fairly weighed, a word or two will help us to that correct estimate of the moral action of Polytheism, as contrasted with Atheism, which it is our object in this place to make.

Any person turning to the "Iliad" at that culminating point of Achillean prowess called "The Battle of the Gods," will find himself in the middle of a scene of celestial antagonism and embroilment, such as seems to render the belief in any consistent moral government from the throne of the Hellenic Olympus impossible. Nothing indeed could appear more degrading to the Divine Nature, or further removed from the severe stability of celestial rule as contrasted with the uncertainty and mutability of earthly dynasties, than such a struggle and collision, contrariety and confusion of Heavenly potencies as this scene presents. When the water-god rages against the fire-god, and the brother and spouse of the Supreme Regent enter the field openly to dispute the commands, and to brave the authority, by virtue of which alone all order and subordination exist in the universe—how is it possible that the faith of any religiously-disposed person should find consolation in the thought of such an anarchy? And is not the attitude of self-contained indifference to all super-mundane powers which the Epicurean atheist maintains, at once more reasonable and more comfortable? More reasonable, certainly, and more comfortable, if that battle of the gods were all of the Polytheistic Providence known to the Greeks, or indeed anything but an incidental scene, worked up into a somewhat melodramatic exaggeration by the feverish fancy of the poet. But behind all this apparent confusion the almighty Jove sits as serene on his throne as the sun behind the wild race of ragged clouds on a stormy day. It is always a difficult matter for a Christian Monotheist to sympathise with the religious attitude of pious Polytheists. Homer knew perfectly well that all this clatter and clash of irate celestial Powers was as futile in the long run to disturb the counsel of Jove, as the barking of an army of curs to bring down the bright sister of Apollo from her sphere. As the pilot that weathers the storms rides gallantly on the rim of a roar of billows, every one of which, to the timid cowering land-lubber, seems destined to engulph the tiny craft in its gorge, so the pious Greek Polytheist, of whom Homer was the spokesman, cherishes an unshaken faith amid all the turmoil of hostile forces, whether terrestrial or celestial, that an Almighty one sits above, whose throne may not be shaken. Neptune may rage, and Juno pout; even Minerva may condescend to an incidental patronage of perjury; but Jove sits apart, on "the highest peak of the many-ridged Olympus;" and where he sits, Justice and Law and the Fates sit with him, as firm as the brazen floor of the firmament which they tread. Those critics who doubt the unity of the "Iliad," and tear it in pieces, as an ill-made Mosaic, will certainly not doubt the unity of this idea, which controls and moulds the whole process of the action.

Διὸς ὁ ἐτελείετο βουλή, and the "Counsel of Jove was fulfilled." * In order to understand the strong back-bone of Monotheism which kept the hostile elements of the Hellenic Polytheism from being dissipated into smoke, we must bear in mind that

* In the invocation at the beginning of what, notwithstanding all the micrologic analysis of the ultra-Wolfians, we shall still wisely believe to be a great poem, the product of a great poetical genius.

the original omnipotence of Jove, which belonged to his character as the wielder of the thunderbolt, was naturally transferred to him as the head of a social order of gods and men; and that in this capacity not only was his authority absolute—like that of the patriarchal chief in early society—but his wisdom as supreme ruler was undisputed, and his kindly disposition as father of the divine and human family as unquestioned as his justice. In him, in fact, centre all those physical and moral forces, which of right belong to the strong and beneficent upholder of the physical and moral order of things in the universe. And so endowed, we rejoice to see him put prominently forward on all occasions as the friend of the weak and oppressed, the protector of suppliants, the advocate of strangers; and specially, as truth in all the relations of public and private life is the cement of society, he launches his bolt with a sharp mission of terror against the head of the perjured person and the traitor. He presides in the forum, and controls the debates of the senate, more appropriately, but not less potently, than the collisions of the battle-field. In a word, he is Divine Providence fully equipped, and may stand for Allah, or "the Great Spirit," or any other name by which the one true God is known among monotheistic races, without offence, were it not for the motley groups of grotesque figures from old traditions hanging to his skirts, which obscure his glory, degrade his character, and caricature his attributes.

There is one other feature of Polytheism which, however ambitious of brevity, we may not altogether omit. It opens the chapter which plays such a prominent part in the theology of the East, the worship of deified mortals. Of this, as it is a distinctive element of Buddhism, we shall treat under a separate head; on its more moderate manifestation in ancient Greece, a few words will suffice here. Now, in the first place, there can be no doubt that whatever wonderful feats of superhuman strength Diomede, or Achilles, or any other highly-favoured hero may perform in ancient story, whether in virtue of his divine birth or of special divine aid imparted for the nonce, on no occasion did the sober-minded piety of the Greeks ever rise into that region of devout intoxication or exaggeration inspired by which the Aryan religionists on the banks of the Ganges contrived with such gorgeous breadth of extravagance to break down all definite boundaries betwixt the human and the divine; only in the case of Dionysus does some strange confusion seem to exist between a sort of Hellenic Noah, the first brewer of sun-breust from the vine, and the great procreant force of nature, working always in the humid element, from which all vegetative and animal life proceeds. The Theban Hercules, though sometimes, in works of art, seen in session with the gods, is no more a god than Romulus to the Romans, or St. Ignatius to the Catholic Church; and if in the wealth of strange legends that have clustered round the name of the son of Alcmene, many scholars of weight have seen an allegorical impersonation of the Sun, and the process of his celestial circuit, this may well be as an accretion to the original Theban Hercules, imported through early Phœnician agency from Tyre or elsewhere, but does not in the least alter the fact, that in the worship which they paid to that hero, the Greeks were perfectly conscious that they were paying honour to a mere man—a typical man, no doubt, and a man looked up to by the whole nation as the ideal of physical strength wisely used and grandly put forth; but a man still—only a step or two of the ladder more exalted than Theseus or Achilles. In fact, the hero-worship of the Greeks was always separated by a distinct and palpable line of demarcation from the worship of the gods. As soon would a modern publisher of an aristocratic Red-book confound a knight of yesterday with a baron of the realm, as a religious ancient Greek dream of elevating a Diomede or an Achilles into the transcendental region of a Buddha or man-god. No doubt there were floating about in the popular mind some strange old traditions regarding the terrestrial sojourn, the birth and even the death of some of the mighty Olympians. But these traditions bore the character of vagrant anomalies and local singularities, well calculated, certainly, to arm the assault of a sceptical unbeliever, here and there, but not in any wise influencing the belief of the mass of the people. The most remarkable of these old traditions, which seem to point to the deification of mortal man as the true germ of the Greek Pantheon, is that with regard to the birth and death of Jove in the island of Crete. The sting of this scandal, which the Church fathers were ever forward to protrude against the Greek idolaters, lay not in the mere legend of the king of gods and men having had a beginning, and having first shown himself to gods and men on a particular spot of earth as their destined regent. Mere birth under a human form did not present itself to the imagination of any pious Greek as in any wise involving participation in the common wants and weaknesses of frail mortality. All the gods of the reigning dynasty had been born in time. Apollo was born in Delos, Hermes in Arcadia, while for the nativity of the Queen of Heaven Argos and Samos put forth rival claims with all the energy that combined piety and patriotism could inspire. The popular theology of Greece was not metaphysical enough to assume an Aristotelian attitude, and inquire curiously whether that which had a beginning might not naturally or at least possibly come to an end. The possibility of the dethronement of Jove from the seat of supreme cosmic government, as in fact his father Kronos had been dethroned before, might be hinted for dramatic purposes, as in the well-known Prometheus of Æschylus, but was no more dreamt of in fact than we should think of speculating on the disappearance of the sun from the firmament to-morrow, which has been gladdening us to-day. But to say seriously that the father of gods and men, the Supreme Immortal from whose throne depends the golden chain that binds all creation with a harmonious unity, to say that this key-stone of all physical reality and all metaphysical consistency was historically a mere man, and a man that had not only been born, but who died and was buried ; this in the ear of any pious Greek was flat blasphemy, and could only have been suggested by men like Epicurus and Diagoras of Melos, or Lucian of Samosata, who wished to bring the Hellenic faith into contempt. And there can be no doubt that the man who first in ancient times boldly and consistently maintained the doctrine that the gods of Greece were all mere dead men deified, meant by so doing to give the popular religion a stab in a mortal part, from which it could not recover. This man was a Sicilian, by name Euhemerus, a philosopher of the Cyrenaic school, and attached in some capacity, we know not exactly what, to the Court of Cassander of Macedon, the immediate successor of Alexander the Great in that quarter. Of him history tells that he made a voyage to the Red Sea, and from that cruise and other marine wanderings returned with a notable budget of sacred inscriptions, *ἱεραί ἀναγραφαί*, from the witness of which he pretended to have found the mortal birth and death of the whole existing dynasty of supposed Olympian gods. This book, as a matter of course, made a considerable noise in the then religious world; and the author unquestionably, had he lived in other times, and under the eye of most religious Athens, might have got hemlock for his sleeping-draught some night, as Socrates did for a much smaller offence, or rather only an imagined offence against the local orthodoxy. His escape, so far as history notes, from all punishment, after such a daring act of public blasphemy, is to be accounted for, partly from the change of the times, but in a great measure also from the fact that books in those days were confined to a very narrow circle—a circle not so wide, we may imagine, as that of the men who read Latin books in Shakespeare's time in this country—and so a little offensive talk and street-logic by a man in the social position of Socrates at Athens a hundred years earlier, might naturally do more to raise the cry of atheism against its author than a big book launched into the literary world in the disrupted state of Greek society that followed the Macedonian conquest and partition. As to the contents of this book, and how far they legitimately seemed to prove a Buddhistic sort of confusion of the human and the divine, no opinion can now be given so long as the book is not before us. Its popularity within a certain narrow range of sceptically-inclined literary men, such as Ennius amongst the Romans, who translated it into Latin, proves nothing. That some heroes of great local significance, as the great Napoleon in France, may, under certain circumstances, by the exaggerated reverence paid to them in popular traditions, have been elevated into the state and dignity of gods, is not to be doubted; but that the Olympian dynasty of Greece, whose elemental significance is so transparent, should as a whole have had only this origin, runs in the face of all probability, and is in no wise to be believed without some substantial proof, very different from that which a few anomalous inconsistencies in the motley swarm of local religious legends affords. We know that in later times mortal kings sometimes took to themselves the title of the god whom they specially worshipped, as was the case with that vile compound of frantic fancies and disgusting vices who once sate on the throne of imperial Rome, called Heliogabalus. And if we suppose that a mortal king as superior to common men, as this wretched caricature of kingship was below it, in the earliest ages of Greek civilisation reigning wisely and beneficently in Crete, had the title of the local god given to him in his lifetime, and after death inscribed upon his tomb, we shall have a theory which explains all the facts of the alleged sepulture of Jove in that island, without resorting to a supposition at once revolting to natural piety, contradicted by the speaking symbolism of the general body of Hellenic mythology, and contrary to all that is historically known of the development of theological ideas in the Aryan race.

So much for this strange chapter of the deification of dead men in ancient Greece. But flinging the speculation of Euhemerus aside, as destitute alike of nobility and of probability, there can be no doubt that the religious homage actually paid by the Greeks to such representative men as Hercules and Theseus (for which they used a special word *ἐναγίζειν* as opposed to *θύειν*), exercised a most elevating influence on the national character. It was not among the heroes or demigods, but among a certain class of the supreme Olympians themselves, that the germs of a most degrading moral corruption were to be found. The priesthood of a worship that could be represented by such a debased sensualist as Heliogabalus might well be exchanged for any sort of virtuous atheism; but the national honours paid by cultivated Greece to such names as Theseus and Hercules were one step in the ladder of healthy reverence that consistently leads up to GOD.

One other remark, and we close. We have talked only of the moral influences of polytheism, as these are in fact the most important. A superstition which, though founded on erroneous intellectual conceptions, works practically in the main so as to cherish the best emotions and call into action the noblest energies of human beings, is always better than the cold negations, blank vacuities, or rabid hostilities of atheism. But there is one danger to which a religion, the growth of mere emotion and imagination is exposed from which its ultimate ruin after however long a period of prosperity may surely be predicted. Man is a thinking animal as well as a feeling animal: his brain, if not able to supply the steam-power which moves the social machine, has nevertheless rights of inquiry and survey which it may not forego; and the breaches in the coherent structure of the theology of Homer and Hesiod were so many and so exposed, that a people far less subtle and far less proud of their wisdom than the Greeks, in the natural progress of the popular intellect, could not fail to use them as irresistible invitations to assaults from the side of Reason, which no weapons drawn from a purely emotional and æsthetical armoury could repel. It is only a question of delay, therefore, not of doubtful issue, how soon the decided monotheistic or pantheistic polemics vigorously started by individual independent thinkers, such as Xenophanes of Colophon, so early as 600 B.C., would ripen into a general revolt, and large defection of the popular mind from the most cherished religious traditions of their race. No religion can stand when it comes into a position of glaring contrariety to the intellectual consciousness of the age.

CHAPTER V.

BUDDHISM.

Μηδεὶς ὑμᾶς καταβραβευέτο θέλων ἐν ταπεινοφροσύνῃ καὶ θρησκείᾳ τῶν ἀγγέλων, ἃ μὴ ἑώρακεν ἐμβατεύων, εἰκῇ φυσιούμενος ὑπὸ τοῦ νοὸς τῆς σαρκὸς αὐτοῦ· ἅτινά ἐστιν λόγον μὲν ἔχοντα σοφίας ἐν ἐθελοθρησκείᾳ καὶ ταπεινοφροσύνῃ καὶ ἀφειδίᾳ σώματος, οὐκ ἐν τιμῇ τινὶ πρὸς πλησμονὴν τῆς σαρκός.

"Let no man beguile you of your reward, in a voluntary humility and worshipping of angels, intruding into those things which he hath not seen, vainly puffed up by his fleshly mind.

"Which things have indeed a show of wisdom in will-worship, and humility, and neglecting of the body; not in any honour to the satisfying of the flesh."

St. Paul. Colossians ii. 18, 23.

WHEN I began to consider seriously the strange epiphany of British atheism or agnosticism, as it paraded itself publicly in the persons of Bradlaugh, John Stuart Mill, Miss Martineau, Tyndall, and others, my attention was naturally called to the fact—which our native agnostics seemed to have a special delight in recognising—that in the far East atheism had been publicly professed for more than two thousand years, and was at present the corner-stone of the faith of more than four hundred millions of the human race. A religion based upon atheism was certainly an astounding fact—a fact, indeed, unintelligible, and according to the common use of language, self-contradictory. To my understanding, at least, it seems as meaningless to talk of religion without God, as to talk of the propositions in Euclid without the postulates on which they depend. But this was not all. Contrary to all human instincts, except perhaps the instincts of that Siamese pair, Mr. Atkinson and Miss Martineau, the Buddhists, we were informed, delighted in the idea of annihilation; and to be entirely blotted out from the world of conscious existences was, to their devout imaginations, the ideal of human bliss. Absurd and abnormal as these notions might seem to be, it was in vain to brush them aside, as one might flap away an army of impertinent flies, or stop the ear to the maundering babble of some adjacent bedlam. Here stood the fact: next door to us at Calcutta in the East, four hundred millions of reasonable beings professing a belief in a doctrine essentially unreasonable, and contradicting, as often as they draw their breath, the primary instincts of all living creatures in this Western hemisphere of the globe. It was a matter manifestly that demanded inquiry; and there was at the same time the best reason to believe that the broad statement of these monstrous doctrines, as it was circulated among the sober Europeans, would require to be modified considerably, perhaps altogether inverted before it could be accepted as a philosophical account of the real state of oriental belief. For not only is it a patent fact that the professors of hostile creeds generally misunderstand and misrepresent each other; but the whole method of religious and philosophical thinking in the East is so opposed to the currency of the logical conceptions in the West, that a fair appreciation of such a phenomenon as Buddhism was not to be looked for in the first instance as possible by Europeans; least of all by the Englishman, who disowns all philosophy, and by the Scot, whose philosophy in that deeper region where it becomes identical with theology, is remarkably rigid, narrow, and unsympathetic. I therefore determined, with the help of Williams's Sanscrit Dictionary, Childer's Pali Dictionary, and a selection of the best original works on the subject, of which the name is now legion,* to get to the root of the matter, as far, at least, as that might be possible to a person not versed in the languages of the Buddhist Scriptures; and, when I considered how truly the spirit of Christianity has been seized by hundreds of thousands of persons who never knew anything but modern versions of the Christian Scriptures, I saw no reason to doubt that I might succeed in the attempt. For though profound philological knowledge is necessary to the interpretation of difficult passages, and the solution of a few knotty points, the main character of a religious or philosophical system will shine out from a fair translation as clearly as from the original Scriptures. Such things, indeed, always are discerned, as St. Paul teaches (1 Cor. ii. 14—16), more by spiritual sympathy than by intellectual analysis. Have the spiritual sympathy, and plant yourself—a thing not to be done without considerable effort sometimes—on the native point of view; and a sensible man will ofttimes come closer to the soul of any religious system

* See "Buddha and his Doctrines; by Otto Kistner," Leipzig and London, 1869, and since that date the articles BUDDHISM and BRAHMINISM, in the new edition of the *Encyclopædia Britannica*, by scholars of note; also the admirable little book on *Buddhism*, by T. W. RHYS DAVIDS, London, 1877.

than if he had devoured all the commentaries of all the libraries. Nine-tenths, indeed, of all commentaries are mere impertinent babble of persons who had no vocation to speak; which, if it were stowed away altogether into an oblivious lumber-room, would clear the atmosphere wonderfully, and save not a little trouble.

Chronology and accurate history are well known to be the weak points of the Hindoo literature: so we must not expect to start with any very well-marked and formally authenticated memoirs of the great Reformer of the Brahmanic religion. Nevertheless, the main facts of the life of Buddha stand out distinctly enough, magnified no doubt through the mist of distant tradition, and worked all over with the gorgeous decorations of an unchastened and unscrupulous fancy, but clearly there—except perhaps to the eyes of some of those Teutonic idea-mongers, whose brains so swarm with ingenious fictions that they have no room left for facts. We live, happily, in a generation, when even King Arthur, once consigned to the limbo of all the myths, is being restored to his personality; and so we may with all certainty take our stand on the fact that the celebrated Gotama Muni, who is now worshipped as the supreme object of veneration by all the Buddhists of the East, was born a prince of the Sakya race in the Gangetic of Hindostan, about 100 miles N.E. of Benares, some six hundred years before our era. The exact date, like the age of Homer, is disputed, and likely to remain so; but, if we follow the Ceylonese authorities, who profess Buddhism in its oldest and purest form, we shall place this Luther of the Eastern Church somewhere in the sixth century before Christ—cotemporary with Solon, the Athenian lawgiver; Thales, the Milesian philosopher; and the Etruscan dynasty of the Tarquins in Rome. His original name was Siddartha; and his father, Suddhodana, as was to be expected, took all possible care that his son should be trained in all those arts and accomplishments which belong to a great Eastern prince and the ruler of a mighty empire. But fathers are often disappointed when they plan the destinies of their offspring, especially when those sons have a large stock of that rare stuff in the human family, whose nature it is to shape circumstances rather than to be shaped by them. In this case the destiny of the royal Celtic saint, St. Columba, was prefigured; the young Siddartha, though surrounded with every splendour that could attract, and every pleasure that could allure, would not be contained within the charmed circle of a Court life. To him a Court was only a splendid confinement, and what the Court called pleasure only a more elegant sort of animalism. He felt himself to be more than an animal; he was a thinker; besides he had a hunger of human love in his bosom, swelling with heavings, to which neither the blaze of gold in an Indian palace, nor the allurements of sensuous delight in a harem of the choicest Oriental beauties, could minister any nourishment. So he broke the golden bars of that prison one day, and told his coachman, Tchandaka, to harness his chariot and to drive out beyond the precincts of the palace, to see what might be found there. Now, the king could not prevent this: but being haunted by a fear from some family prediction that his son might one day manifest a distaste for public life, and desert the throne for a hermitage, he caused the whole district within the range of the prince's possible drive to be cleared of every unpleasant or unsightly object that might possibly divert the thoughts of his son from the splendours and luxuries of a Court life. But all his precautions were in vain. On three several occasions, when the prince rode out, he saw spectacles of human misery, such as could not be seen by a man naturally of the most unselfish character without opening the door to a current of the most serious reflections. He saw—so the Chinese book has it—"in one of the streets the body of an old, decrepit man; his skin shrivelled up, his head bald, his teeth gone, his body bent down. He carried a staff in his hand to support his tottering limbs; whilst, as he proceeded, he gasped with pain, and the breath from his mouth sounded, as it came, like the raspings of a saw." * And then, on inquiry, he was informed by the coachman that this was by no means a singular spectacle, but the common lot of all, prince as well as peasant, who might live unharmed till such time as their life found its natural termination. Whereupon the prince replied: "If this be so, I cannot think of proceeding farther whither we were going to sport and laugh. Turn your horses homeward: let us return to the palace; it were better for me to pass my time in thinking how to contrive to escape, or at least to palliate this end of AGE." On his sec-

* The romantic legend of Sakya Buddha, from the Chinese by Samuel Beal. London: Trübman, 1875, p. 109. This book, though of Chinese manufacture, is founded on Sanscrit traditions, and may be relied on as giving a true idea of what Buddhists generally believe, or are taught to believe, of the great founder of their religion.

ond excursion, he encountered on the roadside—whether naturally or by the glamoury of a *deva-putra*, angel, or genius, does not matter—" a sick and pain-worn man, with cramped limbs and swollen belly, giving evidence of agonising suffering, pale and miserable, scarcely able to draw his breath, and every now and then lying down in the dirt through exhaustion." And this spectacle produced a similar effect. Lastly, on a third excursion, a deva-putra caused to appear directly in his path " a corpse on a bier. Then he saw the people lift up the bier and carry it along, some spreading grass upon it; whilst on the right and left were weeping women tearing their hair and beating their breasts with grief; others striking their heads across either arm; others throwing dust on their heads; others wailing and lamenting, and weeping tear-drops fast as rain, with such sad and bitter cries as could seldom be heard. Was this also part of the common lot? Yes, replied the coachman: peer and peasant, sacred bodies and profane, must equally die. Then finally said the prince: If this be really so, and this body of mine must die, and become even as this corpse, what have I to do with pleasure, or why should I go to the garden to find enjoyment? Turn again, O coachman!

turn again your chariot! and take me back to the palace, that I may meditate on what you have said. Then the prince entered the palace again, and sat silently down and *pondered on death and the impermanency of all things.*" *

I have quoted this vision of the three woes almost at full length, because it shows better than the most cunning style of portraiture could what manner of man we have to do with. We have to do with a man of the most exquisite moral sensibility—a man who could no more bear to see sorrow of any kind, without devoting himself to its extirpation or alleviation, than a hungry man can forbear to crave for food. Hundreds and thousands of people in the West End of London see such spectacles readily, but are not so moved; a passing "*poor wretch!*" or a superfluous sixpence flung on the ground, to be picked up by a half-naked suppliant, settles the score of their pity. They make the round of the Row in the sunshine; eat their dinner with sunset from gorgeous plates enamelled with sky-blue, and edged with gold; and after due potations of champagne, port, or burgundy, as the case may be, sally out, through the dark, to the splendour of a dancing-saloon,

* Beal as above, p. 119.

where they remain, tripping it deftly with the young and light-hearted through the small hours of the morning, till their body, with such prolonged exercitation, is exhausted, but with a perfectly easy conscience. Now, I do not say that these gay people are doing anything wrong—quite the contrary; I like to see gay people; it is natural and healthy to be gay; but what falls here to be remarked is simply this, that these fashionable West-Enders, living from week to week and from night to night, with perfect content, in what is called the gay world, are not persons of Sakya Muni's extreme moral sensibility. The illustrious Prince of the Sakyan race could not see these things and dance. He could not laugh, while his brother was weeping. The sorrow of his fellow-men, as it fell down in big briny drops, mingled with his cup of pleasure, and turned it into gall. From that moment he became a sad and a solitary man. His destiny was now fixed. He must seek a way of escape. What might come out of it he did not know; but he could not remain longer where he was. He must seek in solitude for balm to that deep heart-wound which society might hide, but could not heal. He determined to leave the Court and become after the fashion of Brahmanic piety, a dweller in the lonely glens, a recluse. "Through desire a man having separated himself, seeketh and intermeddleth with all wisdom." So said Solomon; and what the Hebrew king said, the Hindoo prince did to the extreme letter.

This retiring into the forest, and living the life of a pious hermit and mendicant devotee, is the second significant fact in the career of this singular religionist. He was a philanthropist of the extreme type, and a monk of the Oriental type; and, if the first is always a rare virtue, the latter is certainly a not uncommon folly. To plunge from one extreme to another, overleaping the mean of moderation and just equipoise, is the common weakness of humanity, which wise men in all ages have studied to diminish, but have in vain endeavoured to prevent. The rebound from extreme sensuality to extreme spirituality—from wasteful splendour to parsimonious bareness—from the plethora of enjoyment to total abstinence, is exemplified in the lives of hundreds of saints and religious persons all over the world, and need not be commented on here. If even in the sober breast of European Christians such sudden revulsions of feeling and inversions of mortal habitude are not uncommon, how natural that they should appear with gigantic proportions in the over-charged religiosity of the East!

The extreme form which moral mortification and religious self-denial delights to assume in the East will be best understood by observing the procedure of Sakya Muni after he left the palace. The first thing he does is to take off from his royal head-dress the precious Mani pearl, and giving it to the faithful Tchandaka, thus addressed him:—

> "Tchandaka, I now give you this precious Mani pearl, and bid you return with it to my father Suddhôdana Maharâja; and when arrived in his presence, after due salutation, bid him dismiss all grief or useless regrets on my account; assure him that I am influenced by no delusion in leaving him thus, nor by any angry or resentful feeling; tell him that *I seek no personal gain or profit by what I do, that I look for no reward—not even to be born in heaven—but that I seek solely the benefit of men (all flesh), to bring back those who have wandered from the right path, to enlighten those who are living in dark and gloomy error, to save them from the constant recurrence of birth and death, to remove from the world all sources of sorrow and pain—for these purposes I have left my home;* and so my loving Father, seeing me thus rejoicing in carrying out this purpose, should shake off every feeling of regret and sorrow on my account."

After this he draws his sword from its sheath, and cuts off his rosy, curling locks, and, not content with that, causes a hairdresser with a razor to appear, and make a clean shave of all the hairy vesture of his poll; and, to complete the metamorphosis, he takes off his splendid purple robe, and puts on a "dirty and much-soiled kashyn garment." Being thus shorn and disrobed, he took a solemn oath that he should no longer be known as Prince Siddartha, but by no other name than *Muni*, or the Recluse.

Undisturbed by the rattle of busy life, and unseduced by the attractions of sensual pleasure and light frivolities, in the solitude of the forest the thoughtful prince had now full leisure to brood over the sins and sorrows of humanity, and to think out a plan of salvation. Converts of the common stamp do not take long to excogitate their remedy for the moral diseases of humanity: they take it as they find it in the traditional orthodox forms of their country, and, after going through a course of thorough personal reformation, often dash into a fervid apostleship with the ready-made shibboleths of their creed, applied in the lump, and with no attempt at discrimination, to all and sundry of the unconverted multitude. Apostles of this class may be found anywhere in these islands; especially in Scotland, where they make the street corners and the public squares to re-echo with their earnest, shrill appeals to the careless sinners of the passing crowd. But the Sakyan prince had a more difficult work to do. He could not accept the Brahmanic way of salvation simply as he found it; nay, rather, he saw in that whole sacerdotal system a Pharisaic pride, a narrow exclusiveness, a shallow ceremonialism, and a super-subtle theology, which repulsed him; from which certainly he could not hope to educe any catholic remedy for the wide-spread miseries of human life. He had therefore to fashion forth a system, chiefly ethical, but partly also metaphysical, for himself; and this he is represented as having done during a space of seven years, without any help from man or God. His system, if not particularly original in its matter—for moral truth is everywhere the same—was, or at least claimed to be, altogether original in its production. The wells of living water, in his case, flowed altogether from within, were the pure issue of severe and long-continued meditation and communion with his own heart in the leafy solitudes. After having excogitated his doctrine, the next desire, of course, in a character possessed with his grand rage for humanity, was to promulgate the way of salvation to his fellows; but in the threshold of this purpose, he is represented as overwhelmed with blank despair when he thinks of the stupidity and sinfulness of the creatures whom he is attempting to convert.* This was a natural enough temptation, felt no doubt by all, more or less, who have made any serious attempt towards the reformation of their fellow-men ; but men of John Wesley's or Sakya Muni's type will not allow themselves ultimately to be turned back from a great moral enterprise by cowardly considerations of this kind ; and accordingly we find that when he was wrestling with such discouraging imaginations, Maha Brahma and Indra, two of the mightiest of the Hindoo gods, visited him in the forest, and persuaded him forthwith to commence an apostleship for the conversion of benighted mortals. Thus strengthened, he girt himself to the task of world-regeneration. His first attempts were made at Magadha, where, however, he met with little success ; † but at the sacred city of Benares, whither he next bent his steps, he made his first five disciples ; and from that germ the apostleship began to burgeon and blossom forth with notable success. Unassisted at first by the civil power, and, of course, with much opposition from the Pharisaic priesthood, and the devotees of their ceremonialism, the pure moral doctrine of

* "Études Buddhiques," par St. Leon Feer, Paris, 1870, p. 7.

† Feer, p. 25.

Sakya Muni, now called Buddha,* made a conquest of the multitude, like Christianity, mainly by the catholic humanity of its inspiration, and by the noble self-denying character of its author. In the course of time, however, just as Christianity was placed on a strong ground of vantage by Constantine in the year 323, so the great Buddhistic heresy received the stamp of secular respectability from the Emperor Asoka about the middle of the third century B.C.

In this manner the grain of mustard seed, after the usual fashion of all great moral reforms, had grown into a great tree, and might under favourable circumstances have, in the course of time, prevailed so far as utterly to extirpate Brahmanism from the whole district between the Indus and the Ganges; but it was not so. After generations of hateful reproach and humiliation from their upstart antagonists, the Brahmans found themselves strong enough to expel the Buddhists from India, just as Protestantism was expelled from the south of Europe by the combined conservatism of Italy, Spain, France, and Austria. But here, as in the

* The words *Buddha* and *Boddha* are the Sanscrit forms of the Greek οἶδα and the Latin *video*, signifying *knowledge* or *spiritual insight*. Plato's φρόνησις. The German *wissen* and the English *wit* and *wot* are obvious variations of the same root.

obvious parallel of Christianity, persecution and banishment served only to spread the seed of the doctrine, and to ennoble the character of its missionaries; and the gospel of Sakya Muni made moral conquest of millions of human souls through the extensive regions of Ceylon, Burmah, China, Thibet, and Japan, which amply compensated for its total disappearance in its original seats on the banks of the Ganges and the Jumna.

So much for the outward scene, and the external fates of this most notable type of oriental piety. Let us now look steadily on its internal character and moral features. We have mentioned already, what is agreed on all hands, that the Buddistic system must be regarded as a protest against the extreme sacerdotalism of the existing Brahmanic system,* and in this respect there is a perfect analogy between the position of Buddha as a religious reformer, and that of Christ in his antagonism to the Pharisees, as also that of Martin Luther in his opposition to the Roman hierarchy. There is, however, this important difference to be observed

* It is noteworthy, in this view, that in choosing his form of incarnation, the destined Buddha chooses to be born in the secular caste of Kshatryas, or warriors, rejecting the sacerdotal type of the Brahmins. Beal, p. 30.

between Buddha and these two cases: Buddha rejected altogether, or at least ignored, the whole strictly theological foundation of the Brahmanic creed which was his cradle; whereas, the monotheism of the Hebrews, with all its accompaniments, passed unquestioned into Christianity, as did likewise the theology of the Christian Churches, always of course with the exception of some later Roman excrescences, into the Protestantism of Luther, Calvin, and Zwingle. What Buddha preached was a gospel of pure human ethics, divorced not only from Brahma and the Brahmanic Trinity, but even from the existence of God: so that, while his moral discourses come upon the ear, in many respects, like an echo of the Sermon on the Mount, there is one sentence in that sermon which could not possibly occur in any of Buddha's exhortations. "BE YE THEREFORE PERFECT, EVEN AS YOUR FATHER WHO IS IN HEAVEN IS PERFECT"—whereas the constant and consistent voice of the Indian Messiah was, BE YE THEREFORE PERFECT, EVEN AS I, BUDDHA, AM PERFECT. And in this view, we may certainly say that the preaching of Buddha, viewed as to its contents, was not so much a religion as a philosophy; a philosophy, however, published according to popular belief, not by a vulgar mortal like Zeno, or Marcus Antoninus, but by an altogether transcendental personage, or god-man, who, if he did not worship any Being higher than himself, as he seems certainly, according to sacred tradition, not to have done, could not avoid being worshipped by the millions of mortals whom his teaching redeemed, or seemed to have redeemed, from earthly sin and sorrow and shame into a state of holiness, peace of mind, and unspeakable beatitude.

Let us now state under distinct heads the main points of his doctrine, philosophical and ethical; for, though he had no theology, strictly so called, as a thinking man he could not avoid entertaining certain opinions about human life and man's position on the earth, out of which, as from a root, his moral system grew into shape.

And in the first place here we encounter the startling doctrine that existence, at least such existence as human beings brook on this earth, is an evil, not a good. The conditions of human life, according to Buddha, necessarily imply evil; and therefore to get rid of evil we must get rid of human life altogether, at least of human life under its present limitations and degrading conditions. The four evils under which the whole creation groaneth even until now are BIRTH, OLD AGE, DISEASE, and DEATH; and these must be absolutely and altogether swept out of the account, before anything like a reasonable happiness can be expected to arise. Christianity was content, in St. Paul's language, to take away the sting from death, and victory from the grave; but the Indian transcendentalist will not be content with any such vulgar ambition; he must "save all flesh from the fearful ocean of birth and death."* This extraordinary dogma, which sounds as monstrous to a sane ear as the stoical paradox that pain is no evil, and pleasure no good, becomes intelligible only when viewed in the light of the doctrine of transmigration of souls—a doctrine which lies at the root of all oriental anthropology, just as the fall of man does in the theological system of our Christian Churches. By the fall of man, as theologians teach, the human race lies under a curse, and, so long as this curse remains, life, though enjoyed in a low way by unregenerate persons, is in reality a curse rather than a blessing; and becomes a blessing only to those who are redeemed from the curse by faith in Christ Jesus and the moral regeneration produced through that faith. The ori-

* Beal, p. 137.

ental theology, while it abstains from tracing the sorrows of the race to a federal head, derives the sorrows of the individual from sins of the individual committed in a previous stage, or rather many previous stages of existence; and the only way to get rid of them is by accumulating such an amount of moral merit, in various successive existences, as may enable the virtuous person to rise at last above all conditions of sorrowful human existence into a super-mundane state of unconditioned beatitude, in the Sanscrit language technically termed NIRWANA. Seen from this transcendental point of view, human existence, in the exaggerated language familiar to the East, may be said to be an undesirable thing, and a curse rather than a blessing; at all events as only a somewhat uncomfortable stage in a long journey full of stages more or less uncomfortable, and on no occasion creating the feeling of a happy home. What are called the pleasures of life, in this view, are all more or less delusions, of which a wise man should get rid as soon as possible: life itself, with all its gay parade and glittering show, is, from this higher point of view, a delusion; it is all fleeting and momentary, and possesses no permanency which a man can firmly grasp; it is a hollow vanity; and the sting of the curse which belongs to it lies mainly here, that its most vaunted pleasures are its most deadly poisons, and its most florid flush of health a veil for rottenness in the bones.

So much for the curse of human life. How now are we to get rid of it?—only in one way, just as you would get rid of a house on fire; run out by the back door, or let yourself down from a window, as may happen to be practicable. To escape from the miseries of human life, we must as far as possible withdraw ourselves from the great current, struggle, and contest of the world; we must mortify our desires, control our passions, practise moderation in all things and abstinence in not a few, and generally cultivate a lofty indifference to vulgar human interests, and a spirit of serene quietude far beyond and above the turbid tides and gusty storms of passion that fill the hearts of men with fret, disappointment, and despair.

The student of the moral and religious history of society will recognise that he has nothing here but stoicism, tinged with a very strong touch of oriental asceticism, and rooted in certain strange transcendental notions about the pre-existence and post-existence of human souls. But in addition to this lofty stoicism and philosophic indifference to the petty passions and troubles of human life, we have in Buddha the evangelic element of doing good to others—the missionary spirit, what Dr. Chalmers used to call the aggressive attitude of Christianity. Retirement from the world; solitary meditation on the realities of the moral life, and the fleeting nature of all sensuous shows and pleasures; self-control and self-restraint; and active benevolence; these four chapters contain all that is practically significant in the ethics of Buddhism, and which, in fact, do not differ materially from Christian ethics, except in the self-containedness and self-assertiveness of their transcendental stoicism. But it will give vividness to the picture, if we add a few passages of their ethical teaching in their own language. The vision of the three great sorrows which, as we have seen, were the means of leading the Sakyan prince to serious thinking, was succeeded on another occasion by a fourth apparition, which is narrated in the Chinese book as follows:—

"Then the prince, having set out on his excursion, the Devaputra by his spiritual power caused to appear, not far in front of the chariot, a *man with a shaven crown and wearing a Sañghâti robe, with his right shoulder bare, in his right hand a religious staff, in his left hand holding a mendicant's alms bowl, and so going with measured pace along the road.* The prince having observed this figure before him, asked the coachman—'Dear Coachman ! who is this man in front of me, proceeding with *such slow and dignified steps, looking neither to the right nor the left,* with *fixed attention,* his head shaven, his garments of a *reddish earthen colour,* unlike the white-clad mendicants, his alms dish too of a purplish shining hue, like the stone "toi"?'

"Then the Devaputra T'so-Ping excited the coachman to answer thus—'Holy youth and illustrious prince ! this person is called a *mendicant (parivrâjika).*'

"Then the prince asked again, 'And what is the calling and conduct of a mendicant ?'

"The coachman answered, 'Great prince ! this man *constantly practises virtue,* and *avoids wrong;* he gives himself *to charity,* and *restrains his appetites and his bodily desires;* he is in *agreement with all men, and hurts nobody, neither killing nor poisoning any one;* but, *as far as he can, he does good to all, and is full of sympathy for all.* Prince ! for this reason he is called a mendicant.' 'If this be so,' said the prince, 'and he is of such a disposition, drive up to him, O coachman ! and let me speak to him.' This done, the prince addressed the mendicant and said, 'Honoured Sir ! tell me, I pray you, what man you are !' At this time the Devaputra T'so-Ping by his spiritual power caused him to answer thus—'Great Prince ! I am called a mendicant !' 'And what is that?' inquired the prince. 'It is one,' the mendicant rejoined, '*who has left the world and its ways, who has forsaken friends and home in order to find deliverance for himself, and desires nothing so much as by some expedient or other to give life to all creatures and to do harm to none; for this reason, O prince ! I am called a mendicant (parivrâjika, homeless one).*'

"Then the prince, resuming the conversation said, 'Venerable one ! and what is the character of the preparation necessary for arriving at this condition?' (To which the mendicant replied), 'Illustrious youth ! if you are able to behold (or regard) all objects of sense (sansara) [*or the Samskâras, vide Introd.*, p. 505, n.] as impermanent, to think no evil and do none; but, on the contrary, to benefit all creatures (by your life and teaching) then this will lead to the condition of a mendicant; as the Gâtha says—

"To regard all earthly things as perishable;
To desire above all things the condition of Nirvâna,
Done with hatred or love, the heart equally affected,
Freed from all earthly objects of desire;
Frequenting the solitary pits or forests or beneath a tree,
Or dwelling on the cold earth in the place of tombs,
Thoroughly emancipated from all personal consideration,
This is the way to regard the character of a mendicant."'"

Here it will be observed that the ideal of the Buddhist saint is a monk; a feature in which it differs essentially both from Christianity and Hellenic stoicism, of which the ideal was an active life: a reasonable harmony with a reasoned universe, according to Zeno; a faith in the Divine government of the world, working by love, according to St. Paul.

In reply to a seductive band of female beauties, who had been sent by Mara, the evil spirit or Hindoo devil, to turn him from his purpose of a holy life, Boddhi-satva—that is, the hermit-prince with the destiny of complete Buddhaship in his breast,—is represented as using the following language:—

"All those pleasures in which the world indulges
Are sources of sorrow, sin, and distress!
By reason of this, the worldling loses all spiritual discernment;

Clouded with ignorance, he lives in darkness and gloom.
Men are never satisfied with the enjoyment of these things,
But I long ago have utterly discarded them, and escaped from
their slavery.
As a man flees from a burning furnace, or a poisonous drug;
I have long since given up these sources of sorrow.
I have tasted of the water of eternal wisdom;
My heart enlightened, I desire to enlighten others,
And to declare the doctrine of the most excellent law.
But if I were to partake of these polluting pleasures,
Then I should in the end fail to attain wisdom,
For it is by continuing in these deceitful pleasures,
That a man acquires the infection of folly and sin,
Neither profitable to himself nor able to profit others;
I, therefore, desire not these things—I cast them away.
It is these pleasures that burn up all living things,
Even as the fire at the end of time burns the world.
They are perishable as the bubble that rises on the water,
Light as a dream, unreal as a phantom,
Hollow and false, deceiving the worldly-wise;
But the man of true wisdom finds no delight therein.
Just as you see the child with his fellows
Playing and polluting himself with filth,
So is the ignorant and besotted man polluted by these;
He sees the dazzling sheen of the jewelled trinket,
And forthwith there arises in him a covetous desire.
That hair of yours which grows from the brain,
What pollution, sores, and ulcers it generates;
Your teeth, that are secretly shed one by one;
Your lips and nose and mouth and eyes,
They are but as the bubble for permanence.
Your waist and loins, your buttocks and hams,
What pollution is here, proceeding from the blood;
And what impurities, the effect of indulgence.
The man who delights in these is foolish
As one who makes a millstone to grind his own body.
And therefore every one who is wise,

Distinguishing these matters, as I have shown,
Will reject and forsake all such false delights.
He will behold his body, day and night circulating its blood,
As the receptacle of that which is unclean, and find no joy in beholding it.
So it is I see you, standing before my eyes
As a phantom, a dream, an unreal appearance—
For all things spring from connection of cause and effect.
These pleasures are in themselves false and delusive;
By these, men are drawn away from the path of happiness,
And led captive along the ways of misery—
They are as a fiery furnace,
As vessels full of poison—
As the head of an angry snake not to be touched,
The causes of ignorance and delusion and death;
Whoever tampers, then, with these,
Deserting the path of purity and wisdom,
Shall in the end, without doubt, perish in Hell.
So, then, having let go these things, and forsaken them,
I am now free as the air or as space, which cannot be bound with a chain, etc."

After these two passages it seems unnecessary to enlarge further on the special character of Buddhistic morality. That it is remarkably pure, and in much of its tincture and tone closely reflecting the ethics of the Gospel, especially as they are manifested in the organism of the Romish Church, is sufficiently evident. It aimed to be perfectly successful, and, no doubt, in the person of its founder was perfectly successful in achieving the practice of self-restraint, of great patience and endurance, of fearless courage, and victorious volition. It succeeded in the annihilation of all covetousness; by the renunciation of property and women every other abstinence was rendered easy, and the negative morality achieved its most complete triumph; * lust and strife and anger, and all the painful twinges of doubt in the bosom of the unstable and double-minded, disappeared. The innumerable evils that proceed from the aggressiveness of selfish passion, and the lust of appropriation, were cut off by the root; the various forms of cruelty practised by man to man, and towards the brute creation, found no place among the disciples of the pure and perfect Buddha; and, on the other hand, whatever highest pleasures flowed from the habitual exercise of the benevolent affections were theirs in full measure, whose greed was not fed by the desire of accumulation, and whose ambition was not stimulated by the love of power.

We now come to that special point in the Buddhistic doctrine which occasioned its being woven into the tissue of these papers; viz. its alleged ATHEISM. And, in order to clear up this matter, we must start with a distinction in all such cases

* Feer, p. 34–37.

too apt to be forgotten: the distinction between the religious belief and personal convictions of the founder of a creed, and the belief of those who accept him as the prophet of that creed. Sometimes, no doubt, these two beliefs may be the same; as when Mahomet preached that there is one God and Mahomet is his prophet, this sentence contained the pith both of his personal creed and of the faith of his orthodox followers. But the case of Buddha, as we shall see, is different; he was a great deal more than a prophet; a rare, exceptional, and altogether transcendental incarnation of moral perfection; and in such case it might well be, or rather by necessity was, that the creed of the disciples contained at least one important article more than the creed of their master. In what exact terms the historical Buddha expressed his atheism or agnosticism we have no evidence; but the omission of all direct acknowledgment of a great original First Cause, the supreme object of worship, in the legendary accounts, as well as the whole tone and spirit of the sacred traditions afford moral evidence of the most satisfactory kind that Buddha acknowledged no being superior to himself; scarcely, indeed, could have done so, consistently with the transcendental excellence which his followers believed to be inherent in his personality. In the Chinese version of the traditions there is only one occasion on which Buddha is represented as praying to any heavenly Powers; and this occasion was on his entrance on a religious life, when, of course, he was far from perfection. As he left the palace, and bade final adieu to all the pleasures of sense, "he stood at the eastern door with closed hands," says the book, "and invoked all the Buddhas," or, as it has sometimes been translated, the Universal Spirit: "after which, raising his head, he looked up into heaven and beheld the countless stars of the night."* But this text is not sufficient to prove that Buddha acknowledged a Supreme Cause in the theological sense of the word, much less that he was in the habit of offering up prayers to any such god of gods. There were devas and gods enough in the popular belief, powerful devas and devils too, as the sacred legends abundantly show, but they could be no objects of worship to a being of such transcendental excellence as Buddha, rather by their very nature could only minister to him, as the angels to Christ in the Garden of Gethsemane. As a religious reformer, we have

* Beal, p. 131.

said that Buddha was not merely a devotee and a philanthropist, but a thinker and a philosopher, and in this capacity we have it distinctly on record that he either did not admit the existence of what the Hindoos call ISHWARA—a Supreme Creator, —or at least refused to admit such an idea as a fundamental notion in the gospel by which he was to redeem the world from sin and misery. There is a remarkable conversation on this subject between him and Alara, one of the great doctors of the Brahmanic theology, which deserves to be read with particular attention. It is as follows :—

"The discourse then proceeds to a consideration of the power called self-existence (Isvara), and the consequent possibility of *creation*. Bôdhisatwa objects to creation by Isvara, because then there could be no succession of events, no causes of sorrow, no variety of Gods, but all men would regard Isvara as their Father—there could be no disputes about this very subject, whether Isvara exists or not—in short, if Isvara created all things, then all things must have been Good, and there could have been no possibility of evil.

"On this, Alara commends the great wisdom of Bôdhisatwa, but deprecates further discussion on the ground that unless there be a power beyond ourselves capable of creating and sustaining the world, that the great problem of the source of evil or trouble can never be solved; for he said, either Karma or the Body existed first—if Karma was not caused by the previous existence of the body, then who made it, and whence came it? But if the body existed before Karma, then it existed independently of it. In either case there must have been a Creator.

"To which Bôdhisatwa replied, 'I dispute not with you on this ground, but as a man who participates in the great mass of evil which exists, I seek only a physician to give me health, I throw no further difficulties in the way.'

"On this, one of the ascetics greatly commends Bôdhisatwa, on the ground that all religious disputes and controversies, where the object is victory only, certainly lead to hatred and greater evils than any good they can effect.

"'But although,' Bôdhisatwa says, 'I desire not to wrangle, nevertheless I seek a condition of escape that admits of no return to life and its troubles;' on which Alara speaks of his system as teaching this. 'But how?' enquires Bôdhisatwa, 'at one moment you speak of your discipline leading to a definite condition of Being (bhuva), and the next you say it admits of no return—this is strange.'

"'And so it is,' said Alara, 'for this condition of which I speak is that of the Great Brahma, whose substantial existence is one of perfect quietude, without beginning, without end; without bounds or limits, no first or last, his operations inexhaustible, his form without parts or marks—immutable, incorruptible.'

"'But if this be so,' said Bôdhisatwa, 'what becomes of him, and who is He when at the end of the Kalpa, this heaven and earth, even up to the abode of Sakra, is burnt up and entirely destroyed—where then is your Creator?'

"Alara remained silent, with a quiet smile on his lips, whilst one of his disciples greatly commended the wisdom of Bôdhisatwa, but reminded him that in old time the great Rishis all attained perfect wisdom in the way described by Alara—for instance (here follows a list of Rishis), all of whom entered into the brightness of the sun, and attained the straight path.

"'What then is this "entering into the brightness of the sun?"' enquired Bôdhisatwa, 'and if I worship these, how can I admit the idea of an Isvara or Supreme God, who alone deserves worship?' Then the conviction seized Bôdhisatwa, that this system of Alara could not be a final and complete exhibition of deliverance, and his heart became sad.

"Alara perceiving this, rose from his seat and addressed Bodhisatwa, 'What then is the system of deliverance, beyond the one I have illustrated, after which you look?'

"To which Bôdhisatwa replied, 'I seek a system in which questions about the elements shall have no place—in which there shall be no discussion about the senses or their objects—no talk of death or birth, disease or old age—no questioning about existence (bhuva) or non-existence, about eternity or non-eternity, in which words shall be useless, and the idea of the *boundless* and *illimitable* (realized), but not talked about.'

"Then he added this Gâtha:

"'In the beginning there was neither birth or death, or age or disease,
Neither earth or water, fire, wind, or space,
Then there was no need of a Teacher for the three worlds,
But a condition of perfect freedom, lasting, pure, and self-contained.'"

Possibly one element in Buddha's objection to an Iswara, as expressed in this passage, may be only the aversion to the received Christian doctrine of the creation of all things out of nothing, so commonly heard in the mouth of the masters of physical science and other thinking men of the present generation; and this, of course, will still leave room for Buddha being an orthodox Pantheist, according to the common conception of Indian theology. But the passage, unfortunately, affords evidence of a general dislike in Buddha's mind to all theological speculation. "As a man who participates in the great mass of evil which exists," says he, "I seek only a physician to give me health:" that is, I am a practical man, my mission is to preach redemption from the course of sin, by the practice of virtue; and I do not see that curious speculation about the creation of the world can help me in my work. Nay, rather I do see that many learned Brahmins occupy themselves with speculations about Trimurti and other theological formulas, while the world around them is lying in sin and wretchedness. This is somewhat like the tone of our own John Stuart Mill, and men of his school; and no doubt is amongst the most plausible and pardonable forms that the absurdity of atheism or agnosticism can assume. There are other points in this same discourse, which plainly point to an identity of Buddha's negative philosophy with that of the great English Utilitarian. The existence of evil is a stumbling-block to both. "If there had been a Creator, all things would have been good; and there would be no possibility of evil." There is no need of answering this objection formally here; it is manifestly not a whit better than saying that because a man can imagine something which he thinks better in the construction of our existing steam-engines, therefore there was no James Watt. The existence of evil can no more prove the non-existence of a supreme author of good, than the existence of a rainy day can prove the non-existence of the sun. Evil is a mere term of relative inconvenience, and has no meaning in the harmonious totality of the divinely-regulated system of the universe. Another of Buddha's difficulties in this passage recalls Mill: "*If there was an Iswara*," says the son of Suddaohana, "there *could be no succession of events.*" Strange; when he is just the eternal centre from which all successions must necessarily be supposed to proceed: but observe, this is merely an oriental statement of the famous doctrine of invariable sequence, which Mill and his school use as a shibboleth to juggle the idea of a great First Cause out of the world. That all things are connected together by a necessary law of cause and effect, is Buddha's fundamental principle of metaphysics.

> "Whoever, practising the rules of a Brahmana, observes the world around him (tchu-fă, *ye damma*),
> Sees at once that *these things are produced by mutual relationship;*
> Perceiving that the *world around him is produced by this mutual dependence,*
> *He recognises then that all phenomena are but the result of cause and effect.*" *

And in many other passages. Now how is it that in Buddha's mind, as in the system of J. S. Mill

* This seems to be the well-known stanza, "Ye damma hetu prabhasa," etc.

and his school, this notion of invariable sequence and necessary interdependence should connect itself with such an unreasoned absurdity as atheism. Simply thus:—Every popular theology delights in ignoring the chain of what we call secondary causes, and substituting for them the direct action of a God specially intervening and interfering at the call of the believer. Whatsoever is done in the world is done directly by God, at the instance and for the benefit of me, his worshipper. This is everywhere the theology of what our theologians call the natural man; and it is only natural that such an altogether false and degrading idea of the Divine procedure should be met by the scientific assertion of necessary sequence and invariable law. But philosophers like Buddha and Mill, who have the largeness of view to see the absurdity of subjecting the scheme of Divine action in a vast and various universe to the momentary conveniences of a petty individual, should also not fail to observe that an invariable sequence, and a constant dependence, is inconceivable without a persistent inherent or underlying Something which, by its unifying action, makes variability invariable, and dependence not accidental!

We thus see how Gotama, whether from having

been brought up under the influence of a sceptical school of metaphysics—and India has always been fertile in all schools of metaphysics—or from the idiosyncrasy of his own mind, while starting as a religious reformer, had the strange misfortune of being forced to throw behind his back the great lever-power and key-stone of all religion, the idea of GOD. Had he then nothing but simple morality to preach? Was he an Asiatic Zeno, or Epictetus, and nothing more? Could he conquer the world by cold, stoical morality, and sublime asceticism alone? No. He required something more; and he found it in that wide-spread oriental doctrine, to which we have already adverted, THE TRANSMIGRATION OF SOULS. This doctrine, in the mind of the general English reader, is a mere Pythagorean fancy, of which traces are found also among the Jews, at the time of our Lord (John ix. 2); but, in order to comprehend Buddhism, we must seize upon this fancy as a living fact in the popular religions of the East; as part of the very atmosphere of all religious life, and the substratum of all oriental theology. The slightest acquaintance with the common books of Brahmanic wisdom—such as the Hitopadesa—will show how deeply this notion lies at the very roots of the whole moral life of the Hindoos. It was a doctrine, like the virtue of ascetism, which Buddha did not invent, but accepted simply as he found it. Logical proof of such a doctrine there was none; but it served admirably so far to explain the existence of moral evil in the world, and was at the same time a striking and constantly present exemplification of Gotama's metaphysical doctrine of necessary sequence, or invariable law, which, as we have seen in his system, has usurped the functions of the Divine Reason and the Divine volition. And it will readily be confessed, that in the absence of a habitual reference to the Divine will in the exercise of that living faith which St. Paul so philosophically defines in the Hebrews (xi. 1.) there is no moral lever that a religious teacher could wield with more effect than this doctrine of metempsychosis. For see how it works. The life of man on this earth is not an isolated phenomenon; it is the sequence of many lives that have preceded it, by a necessary chain of moral causation, and the precedent of many lives that by the continuation of the same chain of cosmic interdependence shall follow it. By virtue of this chain of necessary moral sequence, the evils and the blessings, or rather the exemption from certain worse forms of evil in terrestrial life, are to be regarded as the retributive consequence of vices or virtues practised in previous stages of existence; as in like manner no vice indulged in here can remain without its propagated seed of misery in a future state, and no virtue can be practised without insuring a certain necessary reward, or necessary issue of merit in some future phasis of transfiguration. The awful power of a propagated vicious tendency, or inherited curse, in the case of certain early Greek families, lends inspiration to some of the most solemn choruses in the Greek drama; and the experience of every-day life exhibits the ugly issue from some paternal sin, marring the features or giving rottenness to the bones of their unfortunate progeny. A habitual realisation of this fearful power of sin and misery to propagate themselves through long generations might prevent many an act of reckless folly, or habit of degrading vice, even with reference to the present life; but if, with the additional horrors of a creeping or a slimy metamorphosis, the consequences of to-day's sin are believed to extend over hundreds and thousands of ages, not in the person of his progeny, but in the very transmuted blood and bone of the offender, the moral restraint arising from such a faith cannot be inconsiderable; nay, rather, will act precisely as the hope of Heaven and the fear of hell act upon the minds of professing Christians. No man would willingly cherish the idea of becoming a pig, or an ass, or a snake, or a crocodile, or a newt, or a toad, or a spider, or a goose, in a future state; but the fear of such an embruted reappearance of self, stands constantly in the eye of the pious devotee of Brahma or Buddha, and works accordingly.

The consummation of metempsychosis, when it has run through its complete series of the most favourable changes, is NIRVANA, or eternal beatitude in the bosom of the Infinite. To the contemplative Hindoo mind the miseries of life present themselves in the similitude of a continual tossing on a very stormy sea; and the contrary of this, which is the supreme object of desire, is a quiet and breezeless haven of eternal repose. The same conception of a state of perfect bliss after death appears in the Christian analogue of an eternal Sabbath—a Sabbath of rest which, literally taken, would indeed be an extremely stupid state, even for the most lazy saints; but which, to active and energetic natures, such as belong to most well-constituted Englishmen, would be a state of intolerable stagnation and uninterrupted fret. The Christian Sabbath of rest, accordingly, is to be understood relatively; it represents a state in which the human being shall be freed from a succession of sorrowful struggles, by which his higher nature on earth is oppressed and strangled; so also the Nirvana of the Buddhists. It is merely the stoical indifference, the philosophical freedom from vain cares and silly joys, the unclouded serenity of a soul living in perfect harmony with the constitution of things; this worked up to its ripe consummation in a future state, and expressed with all the exaggeration belonging to the full swing of Oriental imagination, and the curious subtlety of Hindoo metaphysics. It is, in fact, our *eternal life*, and nothing else, as the following Gathas, or memorial verses, distinctly declare:—

" 'There is one born now amongst men
Who has practised the rules of piety for ages,
The Prince Royal, son of Suddhôdana Râja,
Who has resigned the royal dignity and become a recluse;
He, *desiring to open the gates of everlasting life*,
Is now proceeding towards the Bôdhi Tree.
If you are able to do so, and equal to the task,
Repair straightway and see him there beneath the tree,
For now he is about to cross over to the other side

And desires above all things to save others with himself;
Bôdhisatwa, himself enlightened,
Desires also to enlighten others.' "

And again :—

" 'Oh ! Brahma Devarâja, attend carefully !
I am willing now to open the gate of immortality.
If any will listen, let them come gladly;
Let them hearken to me as I declare the tidings of this Law.' "

And this other :—

" 'I now desire to turn the wheel of the excellent law;
For this purpose am I going to that city of Benares,
To give light to those enshrouded in darkness,
And to open the gate of Immortality to men.' "

And yet again :—

" Then they addressed Buddha as follows—' Venerable Gôtama ! your body is of a beautiful appearance, your face and your eyes round and fresh, and all your senses in perfect accord; you must indeed have found the *elixir of immortality, and the way of life.*'

" Then the world-honoured one replied, ' Ye Rishis ! mock not Tathâgata by calling him " the venerable Gôtama." *Ye are indeed in the way of death, and shall reap sorrow and disappointment by continuing therein; but I have found the way of Immortality, and am now abiding in it.* I am able to instruct you therein, if you will but attend and consider my words, if you will but walk according to my directions; if a *man or woman will leave the world, and follow me, desiring to find that highest condition of a true Brahmana, to reach the fountain-head of such a condition,* then such an one shall surely find it, and arrive at the desired goal; his faculties perfected, he shall cut himself off from further birth and death; and well-founded in his religious life he shall *hereafter receive no other form of temporary existence* (*bhava*). *This is what ye should meditate on.*' And so the Gâtha says—

"'Those five Rishis mockingly spoke of Buddha as Gôtama,
The world-honoured one in pity taught them, saying,
"Let not your thoughts be so proud and high;
Let go that pride of self, and obey and reverence me,
There is no pride of self in me, but perfect self-composure;
I desire to change in you the ground of your destiny,
I, who have become Buddha, honoured by the world,
For the sake of all living things, I would bring this good."'"

We have given these passages at length that the reader may perceive how far from true their assertion is who tell us that the Buddhist finds his highest bliss in the prospect of ANNIHILATION. People ought to have thought ten times before they allowed themselves to father on the founder of a great popular religion any such absurdity. Had Buddha really, like the ancient Hebrews, meant to ignore a future life in the enunciation of his law, he would simply have said nothing about it; but he never would have come forward, inducing men to become his disciples by proclaiming—

"*O sin-laden creatures, and miserable mortals, attend carefully,*
I, Buddha, am now revealed ready to open the gates of ANNIHILATION *to all flesh!*"

What he taught was the annihilation of our wretched limited existence here, like the existence of a poor prisoned eagle in a small cage, as the necessary condition of a participation in the unhampered life of beatified spirits, knowing not the bonds of flesh and blood, nor the fretful distractions of petty terrestrial relations. In interpreting the Nirvana as every other dogma of oriental theology, we must put our sober occidental imagination into training, and bear in mind constantly that the whole phraseology in which their dogmas are expressed is systematic exaggeration and paradox. Perfectly true, no doubt it is, that when Buddha, in a state of transcendental ecstasy, talks of the "absence of all relationship, the destruction of personality, the non-consciousness of an *Ego*, and a condition of mind letting go all thoughts of what exists, and what does not exist," *—such a description of Nirvana, when analysed by a sober-minded European metaphysician, seems to mean absolute blankness and vacuity, or simple annihilation; but what we have to do with, in determining the doctrines of the Buddhist faith, as practically received and cherished by the millions of Asiatic souls, is not the analysis of metaphysical

* Beal, pp. 176, 237, 172, 246, 284.

exaggerations, but the popular impression made by a popular similitude; for Nirvana, like some of our Christian doctrines, though now presented to us as a crystallised dogma, was originally only a simile, such as could most strikingly impress the exemption of a state of celestial bliss from the common woes of terrestrial humanity. And as far as the practical working of Buddhism is concerned, and its effect on the minds of the great believing masses, we must never forget that perfect Nirvana is a potency of beatitude altogether exceptional, peculiar to the Buddhas, and the more saintly of their devotees, and could no more lie within the calculation of an ordinary worshipper, than any common pious Roman Catholic can look for a recognised place in the Calendar along with St. Francis of Assisi, or a place in Heaven on the right hand of the Virgin Mary, who was indeed once only a devout mother in Israel, but is now worshipped by more than one-half of Christendom as the Queen of Heaven and the Mother of God.

So far we have attempted to draw in rapid sketch the main lines of the Buddhistic piety as professed and practised by the great Buddha himself. We now proceed to what for our present purpose is a much more important question; but a question which happily requires very few words for its definite answer. What is Buddhism in the faith of those who now profess the religion—the millions of pious orthodox devotees in Ceylon, China, Thibet, Burmah, and elsewhere? The question we have to answer now is not what Buddha was, according to the best historical results which a careful analysis of the traditions yields, but under what conception is he actually worshipped; for it is from this conception alone that we are entitled to draw an answer to our inquiry. Do the Buddhists as a sect profess atheism? To reach the Buddhist point of view in reference to this matter, we must have recourse again to the great doctrine of transmigration—or rather, that particular form of it which we are accustomed to express in theological language by the term INCARNATION. We stated before that, though by us looked on as a mere man, to the Hindoo conception Buddha is a God-man—a Messiah—and therefore justly worshipped, not with merely heroic honours, such as the Greeks paid to Theseus and Hercules, or the Romans to Romulus. No Roman ever conceived of Romulus as existing before his birth on the Quirinal Hill; but the oriental Buddha appeared on earth, as the Messiah of a perfect law, only after æons of supermundane existence spent with Devas, and other divine personages, in one of the Hindoo heavens. Nor is Buddha the only being of his transcendental kind that has been sent, or will be sent, into this lower world. There are many Buddhas: in the infinity of ages, innumerable; and the orthodox Ceylonese belief with regard to Buddhas may be stated formally thus:—In order to redeem mankind from the slavery of sense, and the misery of sin, from time to time a perfect Being in the form of a man is sent into the world to serve as an example and guide to all who are striving to lessen the evils of existence, and possibly, in the long end, to attain supreme beatitude. These are called Buddhas: they are thoroughly enlightened in reference to all matters of Divine law; and in consideration of this, deserve supreme honour and reverence from men. They derive their inspiration from themselves; their insight in all spiritual matters is intuitive, and their utterance oracular. Of these Buddhas, for the present kalpa, or age of the world, Gotama Buddha, or Sakya Muni, is the supreme; and if there be any Being in heaven or earth before whom all human beings ought to bow down with unreserved submission, as at once the true expounder of the Divine law, and its radiant manifestation, it is Gotama Buddha. Absolutely certain, indeed, it cannot be said to be that this great religious reformer formally instituted the worship of himself: but there is no record of his having set before his disciples any higher object of adoration; and it is in every view, according to Buddhist theology, to be regarded as the highest possible satisfaction to the religious instincts of human nature, that the figure of the supreme Buddha sits enthroned as the supreme object of worship in all Buddhistic temples. According to this doctrine, the religion of the Buddhists cannot in any sense be charged with the absurdities of atheism. The peculiarity of their piety consists simply in the concentration of the feeling of reverence on the transcendental personality of a Divine proclaimer of the eternal moral law; God, as the creator and director of the physical universe, being left entirely out of view. And, though this system is undoubtedly both narrow and inadequate, it has at least the merit of directing the faculty of reverence to an object at once the most worthy and the most practical; and, in this view, there can be little doubt that Plato, who found cause to protest so strongly against the immorality of the Homeric gods, as of most evil example to their mortal worshippers, would have allowed Buddha to pass without censure, perhaps even with a kindly nod of approbation. Neither can the Buddhists justly be charged with the humiliation which arises from the deification of mortal men, such as the Romans practised when they placed Cæsar and Augustus amongst the gods. Not only was Buddha an eminently moral man, and therefore more worthy of worship than the immoral gods of the Greeks; but he was, as we have said repeatedly, a god and above all gods, as the Gatha has it—

> "'Above, below, and through the Earth,
> Amongst all creatures that have life,
> Whether gods or men, Buddha is chief.'" *

So much for the practical atheism of which the Buddhists have been generally accused. The worshippers of a transcendental Messiah, the promulgator of the eternal law of moral rectitude, never can be classed with the deniers of God; they only refuse to complicate practical religion with the metaphysical question as to the origin of the uni-

* Beal, p. 365; and at p. 71 he is represented as omniscient, and seeing through all things in a moment.

verse; from which, by the way, the Greeks also abstained, and were never accused of anything but an anthropomorphic superstition. But not even in speculation is it necessary for a Buddhist to deny absolutely the doctrine of an *Ishwara*, or supreme Creator. Whatever difficulties Buddha himself might have had on this subject, and however averse he was to mix up theological speculations with the obligations of the moral law, the following exceedingly curious statement from a speech made by a Buddhist priest, in the celebrated public debate on Buddhism held at Pantura, in Ceylon, will amply demonstrate that his priests do not consider themselves as floating about amid the reasonless vacuities of a blind atheism:—*

"He (the priest) did not deny a Creator, but admitted that he owned his existence to one; but why should he be allowed to become the enemy of the Creator? which he was now. If any one deserved God's conversion it was he. The Christian theory of a Creator was false, and he will presently explain to them who the true Creator was on whom he believed, and what he says will be borne out even by the Scripture account of the creation. He must say that this part of the Bible was most prudently written by one who was in no way a fool. It was said there that the Spirit of God moved on the face of the waters; and why should this fact have been mentioned, if not to show that the acting of this Spirit on the water was the cause of all animal and vegetable life. This

* A full account of the Buddhist controversy, held at Pantura, August, 1873. *Ceylon Times* Office, Colombo, 1873.

was certainly so. The action of air on water always produced animal life; if a cocoanut, which usually remains on the tree without rotting for nine or ten months, be pierced through, and air be allowed to enter into it, the water inside was sure to breed worms; and so long as air could be excluded from water, there was no generation of any insect. Likewise in this instance, 'the Spirit of God,' as it was called, acted upon the face of the waters, and it produced animal life. The origin of all species was then, even according to the Bible, air, with which was associated heat and water. These three, heat, air, and water, by whatever name known—whether as Brahma, Vishnu, and Iswara, or God, Son, and Holy Ghost—were the identical and only origin of species. These were their only Creator, and him he would worship; and as neither air, nor water, nor heat could produce any beings without the aid of the other, but were co-existent and so closely associated with each other that they could not be said to have separate existences, the Christians were justified in saying that though there are three beings, the Father, Son, and Holy Ghost, yet they were not three Gods, but one God. These, however, were not beings, but states."

This is Pantheism—the Pantheism of Heraclitus, Anaximenes, and some of the other pre-Socratic thinkers of Asiatic Greece; certainly not Atheism.

The above outlines, given as much as possible in the words of the original documents, will, it is hoped, enable the intelligent reader, brought up in a European atmosphere, to understand something of the proper attitude and aspect of Buddhism, as one of the most notable phenomena in the moral history of mankind. It remains only, for the sake of greater clearness and decision, that we give a short summation of the results of our inquiry as to the worth and worthlessness of this phenomenon. And first of its worthlessness.

Buddhism, after making every allowance for its many points of practical excellence, and of happy adaptation to the genius of the East, can in no wise be looked upon as anything but an abnormal manifestation of the religious life of man, being, as it is, built up on the foundation of the following five essentially false propositions:—

(1.) The proposition that human existence on this earth is an evil. This proposition could only be true if God were a devil, and if the general arrangements of the system of life in the universe were such as showed a manifest purpose to produce, and did actually produce, a preponderance of misery; but this is exactly the reverse of the fact. If there are headaches in the world, every head is not always aching; if there are toothaches, every tooth in every head is not always longing to offer itself to the expert wrench of the dentist; if there are rainy seasons all over the world, and whole months of rain in Skye, rain is not the constant product of the atmosphere, as the clouds do not always blind the brightness of the firmament, even in Skye; if lovers sometimes shoot themselves from passion, and husbands sometimes murder their wives from satiety, all men are not always lovers, all lovers do not shoot themselves, and all husbands do not murder their wives, or even weary of their society. Neither Romeo and Juliet, nor Richard III., nor Hamlet, nor Othello, nor the Pelopidan and Labdacidan enormities of the Greek drama, are tragedies that occur every day; rather it is their extreme rarity that fits them specially for popular excitement and stage effect. Larks are shot sometimes by idle boys, or comprehensive providers of dainty suppers for ancient Roman emperors or modern French gourmands: but the shooting is a moment of misery to the lark, while its singing has been continued through long summers of bright breezy sunshine. Existence, taken as a whole, is as preferable to non-existence as light is to darkness, or a glass of cool water or warm port wine to an empty tumbler. To say that existence is an evil, is to spit in the sun's face, because some persons have cataract; or to say that there is no sun, because you happen to live under the shadow of an eclipse. Existence is not a bane, but a blessing; not a sorrow, but a joy; and he lives most wisely and most religiously who knows how to enjoy it, according to its nature, most intensely and most largely.

(2.) The second fundamental error of Buddha consists in his placing human excellence in meditation rather than in action. The hero with him is always a saint, never a king. This is a subordination contrary to the great fact of the universe, and in no wise to be accepted. The world is a work; life is a work; growth is a work; all things are full of labour, and attain to their perfection only by labour. True it is, no doubt, in the order of abstract relationship, thought is the father of speech, and speech is the harbinger of deed; but this abstract fatherhood of thought is a thing in itself absolutely without reality; the mere thought of an orange, though entertained and cherished in the most capacious of fertile brains for infinite ages, will never produce an orange: abstract thought is essentially unproductive. Hence it is that mere thinking in the most highly gifted of human beings never produced anything, except in so far as the using of given materials, according to the dictation of thought, may be called production; but God is essentially productive, or what we call creative, and with him any manifestation of living energy is necessarily both thought and deed.* We cannot, therefore, in aspiring to a divine life, overlook the dignity of the deed, to make an idol of thought. A German professor may do this, with a portentous ambition, amid fumes of tobacco and stale beer, constructing the universe by the stages of a logical process; but it is all vanity: a living world proceeds only from a living God; and though a man may found a metaphysical system, he never can preach an effective practical gospel on such a basis. Religious meditation, when set up as an end, not as an exercise towards an end, can issue only with all the more highly gifted minds in transcendental reverie, but with the great majority in devout torpor and pious monotony.

(3.) In the third place, coming out from his long session under the Buddhi tree of devout meditation, Buddha, as might have been expected from such a beginning, falls plump into the vulgarest of all ethical heresies, viz., that the proper cure for the abuse of our passions and appetites is not regulation, but total abstinence from the exciting cause, and violent extirpation of the appetite. Here our oriental saint goes directly to war with Nature,

* This is what Goethe meant when he put into the mouth of Faust, in a well-known passage, "IM ANFANG WAR DIE THAT."

and has just as much chance of succeeding as in attempting to live without his dinner, or making a railway to the sun. Nevertheless, this device of total abstinence is a very old blunder, and frequently practised, from the apparent directness and certainty of the remedy. Cut off the supply at the fountain-head, and the waters will not overflow in the valley. Certainly. But if all the supply of all the fountain-heads be imperiously cut off, what becomes of your valleys then, and of all the green vegetation there? "*If thy right eye offend thee, pluck it out; and if thy right hand offend thee, cut it off:*" an evangelic text this of the highest value, and the best of all rules for a special case; a case in which extreme diseases cry out for extreme remedies, but which never can afford rational ground for the statement of a general rule. Sane-minded men will keep their right eyes and their right hands as long as they possibly can where they belong. The end of man is not to amputate and to cripple his functions, but to put them forth lustily, and to enjoy himself in the luxuriance of their energy. Morality with all its excellence has no commission to usurp the place of enjoyment. God delights to see his creatures flap their wings in the free expatiation of sweet life. The rule of right is not the woodman's axe to fell, but the gardener's knife to prune ; it is, to use Plato's well-known simile, neither the chariot nor the steeds that draw the chariot, but, only the coachman that holds the rein and applies the spur or presses down the drag, as the case may require.

(4.) The Buddhist, and indeed the Brahminists also, to a certain extent, err in teaching that the natural and necessary boundary between the self-existent and all-derived existence can be overleapt by any amount of human virtue, however faultless.

The confusion of the Divine and human spheres of existence is the origin of much that appears to us so strange in the religious fictions of the Hindoos. For the purposes of fiction, Southey, in his "Curse of Kehama," might use it wisely; but to sober thinking it remains a gigantic monstrosity. It seems natural to pantheism under certain conditions to fall into this error. Spinoza and Giordano Bruno, Timogine, kept quite free from it. Hebrew, Mahommedan, and Christian dualism, of course steer clear of any such portentous imaginations. The tendency in them rather is to depress and discourage the creature by the overwhelming presence of an omniscient and overpowering Creator.

Hence the awful gloom and weighty seriousness not unfrequently associated with Christian piety, especially in its early stages, and with an unkindly environment.

(5.) The last fundamental error of the Buddhists consists in the imagination that the human mind, as essentially reasonable, can ever be satisfied without the faith in a self-existent plastic Reason, as the living root out of which this wonderful whole of things, which we call the world, grows ; in other words that the human mind can rest contented with the conception of an invariable sequence of things without a reasonable substantial ground of all sequence.

It will be observed that this error touches only the intellectual side of Buddhism as a philosophy, and does not necessarily vitiate its practical efficacy as a rule of life. At the same time, it must not be forgotten that man is, as the lawyers say, an *unum quid;* that he has a head as well as heart; and that indirectly the practical efficiency of any religion will be seriously affected, when its fundamental principles are felt to be at war with the primary instincts of human thought. So long, indeed, as thought is suppressed, and education neglected, such a religion may continue to satisfy the masses, and dominate the popular sentiment without serious question; but the moment a cultivated reason is stirred to the exercise of its legitimate functions, such a religion droops. The nobility of its moral inspiration is forgotten in the absurdity of its intellectual assertions, and the blackness of its intellectual negations; for a man will not envy the position of moral saintship in a system, where to be an orthodox believer implies that he is intellectually an ass.

In the view of these serious defects, one cannot but feel considerable difficulty in understanding how such a system should have succeeded, as a reform of the existing Brahmanism; inasmuch as its peculiar doctrines are little more than overstrained statements and paradoxical exaggerations of what already existed in Brahmanism, less the altogether rational recognition of a creative Mind. Any person who will take the trouble to read the opening chapters of the Laws of Manu, translated by Sir William Jones, cannot fail to perceive how much more rational and noble the theology of the Brahmans is than the soulless talk of Buddha about invariable sequence, and unavoidable effects from unexplained causes. We can therefore attribute the extraordinary moral conquests of the Buddhistic doctrine, not so much to its own intrinsic superiority as to its emphatic practical protest against the selfishness of sacerdotal caste, the Pharisaic and ceremonial element, with the extreme penances, mortifications, and sacrificial atonements * thereto belonging, as also fire-worship, and other forms of idolatrous superstition, all of which in Buddha's time had assumed such monstrous proportions as to rouse the moral indignation of society, pretty much in the same way that the public market of indulgences by the Roman popes in the early part of the sixteenth century had prepared the popular mind for the anti-sacerdotal protests of Martin Luther.

In reference to sacerdotal penances and ascetic mortifications of the flesh, it is of importance to observe that, though in the above biographical sketch the characteristic features of asceticism and self-imposed mendicancy seems sufficiently pronounced, there exists, nevertheless, a broad distinction between a system of artificial abstinence and a system of unnatural self-torture; and in opposing himself to such unnatural practices in all

* The Chinese book contains repeated strong protests against the shedding of blood by sacrificial atonement. See particularly p. 159.

forms, Sakya Muni, considering his precedents, and the atmosphere which he breathed, is certainly entitled to a very considerable amount of praise. Bitten as he was from the very moment of his conversion with that rage of plunging into the contrary, which is the natural impulse of all sudden converts, it cannot be doubted that he went personally through a regular course of that curriculum of sacred self-torture which was lauded by the then doctors of the Brahmanic church; but herein, as our modern evangelical devotees in the works of the law, he found no rest to his soul; and hence was led, in the process of devout meditation, to strike out that more moderate form of self-discipline, which, to his high-strained imagination, and set against the orthodox cycle of Hindoo mortifications, might well commend itself as the true *via media* between carnal enjoyment and religious castigation. In order to realise this with all vividness, we shall set down here a curious passage which recites how, in the outset of his religious career, the Bôdhi satwa, or Buddhi *designatus*, in the solitudes of the forest, came upon a company of Rishis,* who were practis-

* In Williams's Sanscrit Dictionary a Rishi is defined *seer* and *saint*.

ing their prescribed austerities, and learnt from them the various phases of self-mortification, as follows :—

"'Venerable brother!' they replied, 'you may ask any questions you please respecting our religious discipline, and we, as far as possible, will explain everything to you in detail. Amongst us there are some who mortify themselves by eating nothing except edible herbs (tsae), or spouting shoots of plants (t'he), or the tender stems of the Nyagrodha tree, or of the Dukûla (?) tree, or of the Kanikala tree; whilst others *eat nothing but the stems of one particular tree* (ekadruma), others eat the excrements of the ox, others nothing but the roots of certain plants, or the mashed fibres of different shrubs; again there are others who take just water enough to preserve life, etc.; some clothe themselves with hempen vesture; others with the fleece of the black sheep; others with grassy robes; others with the cotton of the wild caterpillar; others with the dragon-beard plant; others with deer-skins; others with the rags of corpses, or with filthy rags; some again sleep on boards, some on chips, some on tree-trunks, some on pestle-hammers; some again dwell in cemeteries; others in holes; others under the open heavens; others stand in water; others use fire to their inconvenience; others turn always to the sun; others raise both arms above their heads and keep them so; others sit in one fixed posture on the earth; others cleanse not their bodies from filth; others have their hair spirally-twisted; others pull out the hair of their heads; others pull out the hair on their faces; thus it is these different Rishis practise self-mortification, whilst in turn they give themselves to profound meditation and ardent prayers, and vows to be born in Heaven, or to be born again amongst men."

In opposition to such monstrous distortions and grim caricatures of rational self-control, Buddha was entitled to plant himself as a sort of monkish

Aristotle, placing sanctity in the mean betwixt two extremes; and this, in fact, is what we find him doing in the following remarkable passage:—

"'Ye Bhikshus! who have left your homes, there are two things ye should finally and forever renounce—*all worldly sources of pleasure and bodily gratification, and also excessive mortification of body, which neither tend to self-profit nor the profit of others!*' And so the Gâtha says—

"'Reject and forsake places and modes of excessive penance;
Check and entirely control sensuous gratification;
If a man is able to follow these two lines of conduct
Immediately he will attain the true way of ETERNAL LIFE.'

"Then the Buddha continued his address—'Bhikshus! be assured that I have given up each of these erroneous methods, *and this is the middle path to which I have attained; thus am I enlightened,* thus my eyes are able to see and my mind to know, and therefore I have gained a condition of *rest* (*santi*), and am in possession of complete spiritual life, and have accomplished the acquirement of perfect intelligence, and am now a true Shaman, and have reached *Nirvâna and am perfected.* If then, Bhikshus, ye wish to reach this condition, ye must also use *this middle path* which I have used, *and your eyes shall be opened, and wisdom shall spring up within, and you shall enjoy rest, and reach Nirvâna, and the eight paths of holiness* (As'htanga Marga), viz.—Samyak-drishti, Samyak-samkalpa, Samyagvâk, Samyagadjîva, Samyak-karmanta, Samyagvyâyâma, Samyak-smriti, Samyak-samâdhi. This, Bhikshus! is the middle path, which having attained to, my eyes are opened, and *I have found rest,* etc. To this, therefore, ye ought to tend; as the Gâtha says—

"'Because of these eight paths leading aright,
A man casts off the trammels of life, death, and fear,
Having entirely got rid of all the effects of Karma,
Through eternity he shall no more receive migratory existence.'"

In preaching thus, the Hindoo reformer could not but appear as the spiritual friend and deliverer of many pious souls, who, to use the language of the apostles of Christianity, had for ages been groaning under a yoke which neither they nor their fathers had been able to bear; and we may with perfect truth recognise in him a certain spiritual brotherhood with the great Western preacher who taught that in Christ Jesus there is neither circumcision nor uncircumcision, but a new creature.

(2.) But the principal element which in the end secured to Buddha such a remarkable triumph over the established religion of his country, beyond all doubt was the extreme innocency, purity, benevolence, and disinterested philanthropy of himself and his immediate disciples. It was the fervour of the missionary spirit that conquered in the case of Buddha, as it has so often done in the case of Christian missionaries. In all times and in all places love is the key to the human heart, and the great weapon in all moral battles; in all high-minded, self-devoting apostleship, there is a contagion which, when aptly applied, the human heart can no more resist than gunpowder can disown the spark which ignites it. The admiration produced by the noble and altogether unworldly self-renunciation of the young Sakyan prince comes out in several passages of the Chinese book, and notably in the following :—

"Then another Brahman of the company, having observed the grace and force of Bôdhisatwa's manner, addressed one standing by and said, 'Venerable one! it seems to me that this is no other than a child of Heavenly birth, thoroughly acquainted with the human heart, who now by means of this expedient desires to accomplish some illustrious purpose. For why? we find that in the world men speak thus—"I must nourish and bring up my sons in order that when they grow up they may help to establish and benefit my family name, in buying and selling and getting profit for me, so that when I am old I may be able to devote myself to religious inquiries and practices." It is *thus men generally* think and speak, they *have a reference in all they do to their own advantage. But with this one it is not so, he seeks the good of others and not his own, he provides nothing for himself.*'"

And again :—

"Then one of the Manava youths, a disciple of Alara, broke out into the following eulogy, his hands clasped together in token of reverence, as he addressed Bôdhisatwa, 'Oh! rarely seen is such wisdom as thine; *in olden times indeed many kings, satiated with worldly pleasures, have forsaken their homes, and sought for religious perfection in the solitudes; but thou! so young and in the vigor of your age, to give up the certain enjoyment of Royalty, and to prefer the harshness of a life in the desert—the companion of wild beasts, and the unfettered birds! wonderful indeed is this!*' And now, Alara, addressing Bôdhisatwa, said, 'Venerable Sir! seeking what way and in pursuit of what object, have you bent your steps hither?'"

All this, and the general tone and scope of Buddha's teaching, stripped of the grotesque bedizenment in which it is presented, plainly shows that Buddhism triumphed, just as Christianity triumphed, fundamentally because in all moral battles, love and humanity, with their innate expansiveness, will always triumph over the narrowness of self-contained pride and unsocial aggrandisement. If there be in the realm of physical forces a natural selection, which, as Darwin teaches, necessarily leads the stronger and more healthy type to overwhelm the feeble and the diseased, not less certainly is there in the moral world a law of moral selection, which forces lies to retreat before truth, as night yields to the day, and Malignity to grind her teeth and to spit her venom before Benignity in vain.*

How far the Buddhistic religion, notwithstanding the high and evangelical tone of its morality, may have proved a great practical failure, I do not feel in a condition absolutely to declare. Every religion that starts with a high and unworldly

* Even a zealous Christian missionary allows that Buddhism in the East has proved "more of a blessing than a curse," and is to be regarded historically as a notable engine of social elevation. Three lectures on Buddhism by the Rev. Ernest T. Eitel. London, 1871, p. 10.

ideal, must in one sense prove a failure as soon as it becomes a fashion and tradition to profess it. Christianity, in this sense, has proved a tremendous failure; and Buddhism, of course, could much less escape a similar doom, in proportion as it was less human in its sympathies, and more removed from common life in its practices. For Buddhism must fail, not merely like Christianity in so many places, by outstriding the moral ambition and transcending the moral capacity of its professors, but by insanely attempting to override the common instincts of humanity, and disown the primary conditions on which human creatures are created. The necessary result of such an overstrained system is a double morality, a morality of artificial sanctitude combined with natural stupidity, and sometimes systematic hypocrisy in the priests and a morality of worldly accommodation, external observances, and customary indulgences in the people, combined with the silly ceremonial or barren formalism of a religion which is not a reasonable service. It might have been expected, indeed, that Buddha, in protesting against the exclusiveness of caste, and, like Christ, preaching the gospel to the poor, might have prevailed to deliver his followers from the burden of supporting a number of idle persons performing a routine of silly mummeries, called priests ; but religious teachers must exist ; and, whether formally claiming the privileges of caste or not, they will not fail to organize themselves into a strongly knit association of persons exercising sacerdotal powers, so long as an artificial ideal of sanctity is maintained, and the people are not sufficiently instructed to understand that true religion is not a separate business administered by a separate profession, but a common principle of action inspiring all breasts, and giving elevation to all forms of social energy.

I subjoin two passages from recent writers, exhibiting what, no doubt, is the dark side of practical Buddhism (for the light side we cannot expect to be very patent to English residents and foreign missionaries), but which still, I fear, must be accepted as a true picture, so far as it goes :—

"It is specifically urged against the doctrines of Fo, by the Confucians, that they unfit men for the business and duties of life, by fixing their speculations so entirely on another state of existence as to lead some fanatics to hang or drown themselves in order to anticipate futurity ; nay, two persons have been known to commit suicide together with the view of becoming man and wife in the next world. The priests are sometimes accused of employing their superstitious arts in seducing women ; societies of women, at least, called Ny-Koo, a species of nun or female devotees, are encouraged by them. The tricks occasionally made use of by the priests, resemble the practices of the fakirs of India. Le Comte tells a story of a bonze, who went about in a vessel stuck full of nails (something like that in which the Carthaginians are said to have shut up Regulus), and pretending that it was a merit to relieve him from his pain, he sold these nails to the devout at so much per head.

"Their notion of abstraction, or quietism, seems to aim at getting rid of all passions, even of thought itself, and ceasing to be urged by any human desires: a species of mental annihilation. Certainly, to judge of its effects on the priests, the practice of Buddhism appears to have a most debasing influence. They have, nearly all of them, an expression approaching to idiotcy, which is probably acquired in that dreamy state in which one of their most famous professors is said to have passed nine years, with his eyes fixed upon a wall! They say, with reference to their systems of moral retribution, that what a man receives now is an indication of his conduct in a former state; and that he may augur his future condition by his behaviour in this life. The merit, however, would seem to consist as much in inaction as action: in the abstinence from evil, or the mere self-infliction of pain, rather than in the practice of good. They make up an account with heaven, and demand the balance in bliss, or pay it by sufferings and penances of their own, just like the papists of Europe." *

The next witness is from an intelligent Scotsman who resided eleven years in Ceylon :—

"During the continuance of the festival, the priests of Buddha seemed to think it incumbent on them to perambulate the town with their begging dishes, and to go through the ceremony of receiving alms. They moved on slowly with their fans before their faces, occasionally halting to receive whatever food was offered them, but not asking for it. It appeared to me that this was more of a temporary penance than a regular practice, although to live by alms is enjoined by the rules of their order. Their sleek faces

* "The Chinese," by J. F. Davis. London: Knight, 1840, p. 219.

and sly looks spoke of better fare procured elsewhere with less trouble and more certainty than wandering in heavy rain through Kandy, and waiting for supplies from the more devout portion of those professing the Buddhist religion." *

Very sad, all this! but it could not be otherwise; for neither in Ceylon nor in Canton, or elsewhere, do men gather grapes of thorns or figs of thistles. So long as reverence is not firmly wedded to reason, religion can never exist without a certain alloy of nonsense, nor morality become altogether identified with Nature in a creature with whom Truth is the one proper law, Love the one seemly inspiration, and Energy, according to truth and love, the chief end of his existence.

* "Eleven Years in Ceylon," by Forbes, vol. i. pp. 312 and 301.

CHAPTER VI.

THE ATHEISM OF REACTION.

Φάσκοντες εἶνα σοφοὶ ἐμωράνθησαν.
ST. PAUL.

ACTION AND REACTION ARE EQUAL AND CONTRARY: so I was taught many years ago in the Natural Philosophy class, Marischal College, Aberdeen; and through a long life have had constant occasion to note the general correctness and wide applicability of the sentence. It is the nature of every force, in a world made up of a rich variety of opposing forces, either to be stopped in its action altogether—as the advancing tide by a rocky coast—or to be sent back on its own traces, as we see in the heavings to and fro of a great crowd of people, when the over-pressure in one direction produces a stronger pressure in the opposite direction, till some sort of comfortable adjustment be achieved in which the jostled thousands may breathe freely. So it is exactly in the great intellectual and moral movements of society, which constitute the marked epochs of history. It is impossible to live the space of a single generation in the world without seeing striking instances of this sort of propulsion and revulsion of sentiment pass before our eyes. What has become now, for instance, of that grand burst of classical enthusiasm which, some half-a-century ago, sent Lord Byron and some score of adventurous Britons on the romantic expedition of driving the Turk out of Greece, and reconstituting a kingdom of Greek-speaking men, beneath the white majesty of the Periclean Parthenon? The Greek is now, in John Bull's estimate, only a merchant of very sharp practice, and nothing more. Our old ally, the Turk, has suffered under a similar swing of the pendulum; and the Russophoby of some thirty or forty years ago is now veering round to the Russophile point of the political compass, and accustoming itself to look with a grand cosmopolitan sympathy even on the probability of a speedy settlement of the great Arctic bear on the tip of the Golden Horn. Take, again, the department of Art. Look into any of the great English cathedrals, and say what you see there. The internal walls of an edifice of an essentially Gothic type stuck over all round with monuments and other decorations, in the pure Greek, or composite Italo-Roman style, as unlike to what one should expect there, as a tree would be which, growing up so high on the type of a white-stemmed birch, flinging its tresses lightly on the breeze, should suddenly alter its style, and end in the ruddy arms and dark-green needles of a Scottish pine. What was the cause of this? Simply the reaction from the Gothic style of the Middle Ages, and the rage of admiration which possessed Europe for everything that could boast the prestige of Greek and Roman kinship. In the architectural books of those days, you will find the Gothic style of church, college, or cottage, on which we now pride ourselves, simply noted as a barbarism, which a cultivated taste will look at to avoid. And a similar phenomenon may be observed in every form of physical, moral, and intellectual life; so that we may almost lay it down as a historical proposition of universal validity: *every social state sooner or later begets its contrary;* and that not only by the natural power of recoil which we see in springs and other elastic bodies, but from the mere love of novelty. In poetry this is particularly remarkable. When Pope's poetry of sparkling antithesis, sonorous swell, and shrewd condensation had enjoyed its day, no genius, however powerful, could have impressed the British public in a similar degree, had it presented itself in the same form. A quite new form of conceiving and picturing the grand old truths of Nature was required; and this the public, after a short season of ebb, received in large flood from Cowper and Burns, Wordsworth and Shelley, Byron, Scott, and others. An influence which acts so potently and spreads so widely in the domains of politics, poetry, and the arts, could not fail to show itself in theology. If our maxim be true that all action has a tendency to go into the extreme, and that every social state sooner or later begets its contrary, then in the movement of public opinion, and the revolutions of social sentiment, it may sometimes happen that *religion begets irreligion, and orthodoxy becomes the father of heterodoxy*—a paradoxical thing, no doubt, to say, but nevertheless quite true, when rightly understood. And to understand it rightly we must remember the great Aristotelian maxim, that any good misapplied, or applied without limitation is an evil; and that the great movements of human society called reforms, revolutions, and revivals, take place generally after the fashion of floods in water, or strong pressure in a crowd, which in the nature of the case tend to excess, and cry for limitation. This is what Solomon meant when he said :—"Be not righteous overmuch : why shouldst thou destroy thyself? Be not wise overmuch : why shouldst thou die before thy time?" When we say, therefore, irreligion is ofttimes begotten from religion by a natural reaction, we simply mean that piety exhibited to the world in a graceless, clumsy, and unpleasing aspect, or with an obtrusive forwardness, or a feverish impatience, or with a dictatorial imperiousness, a stern harshness, or in any other form destitute of the proprieties and the pleasantness of well-conditioned nature, will have itself to blame if an effect is produced the very contrary to that desired. Shut the door with a bang and it opens, and perhaps strikes you on the face. Do you think that strange? No. Then as little be surprised if certain stiff, and rigid, and bristling forms of theological orthodoxy should produce heterodoxy; nay that even theism, the only reasonable theory of the universe, in the blundering fashion in which you state it may possibly produce atheism, the most unreasonable of all theories. Every exaggerated statement, or offensively-worded proposition—even when there is fundamental truth in the matter—cannot escape from a double evil consequence; it not only irritates the person whom it was meant to convince, but it supplies him with an argument of which he will not fail to make a dexterous use. And in this way, every abuse in religion, and every crude conception and rash assertion in theology, has a natural tendency to produce irreligion, and to end, where other influences co-operate, in practical or speculative atheism. It will be the business of this paper to look at this special phase of atheism, somewhat in detail.

Let us take a glance, in the first place, at the greatest event in the moral history of modern Europe—the Reformation, or Revolution, as it should rather have been called, of the Christian Church in the sixteenth century. This terrible ecclesiastical earthquake—for so we may quite soberly call it—was unquestionably a reaction from the excess of sacerdotal assertiveness, and the abuse of ecclesiastical power, in the latter centuries of the Middle Ages. How did this excess show itself? and in what shape did it give sharp offence to the delicate conscience of Martin Luther, and rouse his sleeping wrath into a thunderstorm of holy indignation? Plainly by his parading the public places, and marching through the highways of Christendom with a sacerdotal gospel of salvation by works: and what sort of works? Of course, conventional and arbitrary works, penances and payments of various kinds imposed by authority of the all-powerful clergy, and having little or nothing in common with the morality of a pure life, and a noble character, which is the characteristic glory of the gospel of Christ, as contrasted with the great mass of polytheistic religions, the strange growths of sensuous excitement and transcendental imagination. Against this abuse Luther protested exactly in the same way, and with similar effect, as St. Paul protested against the ritualism, ceremonialism, and externalism of various kinds, on which the Jews raised a meritorious claim of preference before the general Father of the human race. Of meritorious preferential claims, especially when founded on works of a conventional, arbitrary, and institutional character, there can be no mention before God: "the just live by faith"—faith in that Saviour who preached a perfect ideal of morality, existing always as a measure of attainment, but never as a claim of merit. This great doctrine, preached by St. Paul and Luther, and stated with most effective emphasis in the Epistle to the Romans and the Galatians, has saved the world twice—once from the cumbrous and narrow-minded ceremonialism of the Jews, and again from the despotic and soul-stupefying sacerdotalism of the Romanists. So far well. But the miner's son of Eisleben was a man of too volcanic a temper to be able to keep the reaction which he roused within the bounds of salutary moral therapeutics. The sacerdotal ossification into which he had cast the blood of a new life, found itself confronted with a fever of individualism in various violent and grotesque manifestations, removed not less from the imperious dogmatism of the Roman popes than from the moderation, humanity, and sound-mindedness which characterised the gospel of St. Paul: and anarchy and confusion, with the braying of a theological ass here, the cackling of a clerical goose there, and the ravings of a sectarian madman in a third quarter, began to show face to such a degree that sensible and quietly-disposed men, like Erasmus, became seriously alarmed before the spirits they had conjured up, and retreated, with a devout timidity, into the sacred ark of the old Catholic Church. But even with all these extravagances, the simple doctrine of Luther, that the just shall live by faith, was exactly, as in the time of St. Paul, forthwith subjected to a misunderstanding, which even now works perniciously in some Protestant churches, and breeds, in a certain class of minds, a distaste for Christianity which may naturally fall into general irreligion, and even rush blindly into the blank vacuities of atheism. This abuse consists simply in planting faith antagonistically, not to ceremonial, conventional, and statutory work, or to work set up as a meritorious human claim, but to virtuous works generally; a perversity sufficiently evident to any one who will seriously study the eleventh chapter of the Epistle to the Hebrews, where faith is defined as a practical conviction of the reality of God's moral government, and a conviction manifesting itself naturally and necessarily in a course of virtuous, self-sacrificing, and heroic conduct, such as we see in the lives of all the great statesmen, patriots, and prophets which the common consent of mankind has set up for models of imitation in the great Pantheon of humanity. Thus Christian faith and works are not opposed, but are essentially one; or, at least, two, of which the one as necessarily produces the other, as the fruit of a flower is developed out of the blossom. How far this misapplication or one-sided statement of the great Protestant doctrine of salvation by faith has worked in producing, in the way of reaction, a prejudice against Evangelical preaching altogether, those whose ears are open to what is felt and said by some of the most serious thinkers in the midst of us, will have no difficulty in perceiving. Persons who reject Christianity, or, like Mr. Atkinson and Miss Martineau, openly profess a sort of atheism or agnosticism, do it not unfrequently on the ground that Christianity has failed in its mission; it has not converted the world,*—and no wonder; for a religion that preaches salvation by faith and not by works, naturally directs attention into a transcendental region of what has been called "other-worldliness," and far away from all those practical plans for the improvement of the world and the progress of society which fall under the profane category of good works. Of course we do not say that this way of stating the case against the religion of the gospel is in any case to be taken as a true account of the whole matter; so far

* Letters of ATKINSON and MARTINEAU, p. 172.

as my experience has gone, the most zealous Christians, even when narrow-minded and bigoted, as they too frequently are, can bear comparison, in respect of good works, with the most decided and thorough-going of the atheistical or agnostic class; but that there is some truth in it, and a truth, which it behoves Christian preachers most seriously to consider, I have long been convinced. There is a style of preaching, the unpractical and unfruitful nature of which has a tendency to drive persons of a practical turn of mind directly into irreligion and practical atheism: they see that something ought to be done for society which the Church will not do, or the Church cannot do; and, therefore, they resort to other and, it may be, antagonistic agencies. Akin to the one-sidedness of that theology which preaches faith rather as a means of justification from past guilt, than as a habitual formative principle to mould the character and to direct the life, is the sort of rampant orthodoxy which delights in doctrinal exaggeration of mysteries, and which is never so happy as when it can plant itself behind the broad shield of unintelligible formulas and traditionary shibboleths, to pluck Reason by the beard, and bid open defiance to that grand principle of the Scottish philosophy called common-sense. Those who excite to an atheistical reaction in this fashion, sin even more grievously against St. Paul's doctrine in the Hebrews than those so-called federal theologians who exhaust their whole thought in the inculcation of a faith, whose principal object is to shake off the burden of inherited guilt which lies upon us from the sin of our primal father in Paradise. For there is unquestionably a very strong element of a moral nature in this faith ; and therefore in so far it is evangelical. But that other faith of cataphract orthodoxy mailed in triple brass, of which we now speak, is a purely intellectual affair, and as such altogether outside the pale of that saving faith, by which sinful souls under gospel preaching are dragged out of the mire of sensuality, and the slavery of degrading fashions, into the glorious liberty of the sons of God. No doubt, as St. Paul distinctly enough states, there must be a root of firm doctrinal belief at the bottom of all Christian faith, or rather, we might say, of all practical faith : for who will leap from his bed and rouse the town at midnight, and cry for water, and apply his hand to the forcing-pump, if he does not believe that the house is on fire ? Who will prepare to bury his friend, if he does not believe that he is dead ? Who will sow seed in spring, if he does not believe that it will bear a rich crop of beneficent fruitage in the autumn? "He that cometh to God," therefore unquestionably, "must believe that He IS, and that He is the rewarder of them that diligently seek Him." But this is quite a different thing from saying that whoso believeth not this or the other dogma about the Divine nature shall, without doubt, be eternally damned. Here we have a usurpation of the rightful throne of an essentially moral faith, by a faith purely and avowedly intellectual, and which has just as little to do with the evangelical faith which worketh by love, as any proposition in Euclid has, about the qualities of triangles, or any Algebraic formula about the relations of numbers. To any man, with or without lawn sleeves, who stands up in a Christian congregation, and fulminates damnation to poor sinful mortals on such grounds, there is only one reply to be made: —"Ye know not what manner of spirit ye are of." The spirit from which damnatory declarations of this kind proceed is a mingled spirit of ignorance, conceit, presumption, insolence, and pedantry; and has more to answer for in the way of creating atheism, than any other fault of Christian preachers that has come under my observation. Against declarations of this kind, however solemnly made, and however traditionally hallowed, the moral and intellectual nature of the most soundly-constituted minds rises up in instinctive rebellion ; the intellectual nature, because the propounding of dogmas in a scholastic form about the nature of the Supreme Being, shows an utter ignorance of the proper functions and limits of the human intellect; and the moral nature even more emphatically, because to make fellowship in any religion conditional on the merely intellectual acceptance of an abstract proposition addressed to the understanding, is to remove religion altogether out of its own region, where it can bear fruit, and to transplant it into a soil where it can show only prickles that fret the skin, and thorns that go deeply into the flesh—a procedure, in fact, not a whit less absurd than to plant potatoes on bare rocks, and expect that they shall grow, or to fling a flouncing fish upon the dry beach, and demand that it shall swim.

So much for the caricatures of faith which, being mistaken for the genuine portraiture, have a tendency to drive persons of a hasty temper and a superficial observation into an anti-Christian attitude, or even right off into the dreary silences, blank vacuities, and blind necessities of speculative atheism. But it is not only in their way of presenting faith generally, but in their rash and unreasoned statement of special points of Christian belief, that our theologians have greatly erred. What, for instance, made a greater noise in the world of theological doctrine at one time than the five points of the Synod of Dort, which caused the persecution of Grotius and the noble company of Arminian doctors in Holland? Wonderful subtleties and windy battlements, all of which no man of sense at the present day thinks worthy even of a passing regard. Why? Because these famous five points all relate to God's decrees, and not to man's work; and therefore are properly left to God, while we attend to our duty. No doubt St. Paul has laid down the doctrine of divine decrees grandly in the Epistle to the Romans; and he was obliged to do so, in arguing with the Jews, who nourished the conceit that they were a chosen people, to whom, by preference, God must communicate his saving knowledge, while the rest of the world was allowed to sleep in the darkest ignorance, and to rot in the lowest sensuality. To beat down such a narrow-minded conceit and presumptuous notion of heriditary privilege, the great Apostle was obliged to state the doctrine that, though all privilege comes from Divine decree and special Divine favour, it does so, not for the purpose of creating a ground of vain boast on the part of the favoured people or person, but for the purpose and with the effect of opening up a higher sphere of action, with a more serious responsibility; that is to say, in other words, he taught the doctrine of predestination and reprobation, not in the way of arbitrary selection and rejection, as the extreme Calvinistic theologians have rashly taught, but in the form of a necessary law in the moral world, according to which divinely conferred gifts—and all gifts come from God—when abused, lead to forfeiture and loss, when improved, to greater gain and more distinguished privilege. According to this common-sense view—and it is the plain and obvious drift of the Epistle—all the fierce and bloody gladiatorship between Calvinists and Arminians about the orthodoxy of the five points of a scholastic doctrine of Divine decrees was an episode in the great epos of Christian life, interpolated by men who were as remote from the broad, practical drift of the Pauline gospel as they were devoid of the common feelings of humanity. St. Paul, the innocent occasion of all this barbarity, would have made short scores of their interminable debates and overbearing dogmas. "Gentlemen," he would have said, with that fine instinct of practical sagacity which directed all his teachings, "Gentlemen, you beat the wind: Necessity is true, because nothing can escape the wide embrace of the Divine Sovereignty: Liberty—that is, liberty within certain limits, is a fact—because the common instinct of humanity proves that it is so: you must believe both, and quarrel about neither. But believe not metaphysically or scholastically, but practically, and in such a way as the Jews, my countrymen, did not believe, and suffered accordingly." I have brought forward this matter specially because, though the five Calvinistic points are now scarcely known by name to many well-educated persons, they are all involved in the catechism used in the elementary schools of Scotland, and have to my knowledge occasioned no small amount of misery and soul-torture to young persons beginning seriously to look into the great truths of religion and morals. Thoughtful young persons in Scotland, under the influence of such Calvinistic teaching, will be found vexing and perplexing themselves most lamentably about their special election or reprobation; than which a more unprofitable exercise, or more out of place, cannot well be imagined. All such questions belong either to the past or to the future, and as such lie in the bosom of the Infinite. Man is a creature of the present; and he must strike the nail upon the head in the special work before him, not because he has been predestinated to do so, or because it may turn out after trial that he has not been predestinated to do so, but simply because it is before him. With the decrees of God, however prominently they may stand in the vestibule of the Assembly's Catechism, a young man on the threshold of life has no more to do than he has with the creation of the world, or with the consummation of all things.

Another dogma, with the inculcation of which the Calvinistic theologians have done good service to the anti-Christian tendencies of some respectable classes of the community, is the doctrine of original sin. With regard to this, Coleridge, who, in other matters, spoke vaguely enough, said the proper thing in a single word—"Original sin is not a doctrine, but a FACT." So stated, it is only what we see every day before our eyes, and can, of course, form no special objection against Christianity. That out of good seed a good plant will grow, and out of bad seed a bad plant, and that from generation to generation, till the action of fresh favourable influences cause a change, is a principle of which the exemplifications are as wide as the range of organized life upon the globe. Books have been written on hereditary virtues and hereditary vices ; and every family portrait-gallery, going back for long centuries, notwithstanding strange variations, arising naturally from cross affinities, will revert now and then to a striking trick of the original type. So far, so well. But now in comes our cataphract theologic doctor, with his host of dogmatic exaggerations, and thunders out his dogma of inherited GUILT, at which straightway an honest thinker's whole moral nature bristles up in rebellion. Moral merit and demerit are in the very nature of things personal ; to imagine their transference is to destroy their definition. If every baby when born, in virtue of an act of transgression committed some six or eight thousand years ago by the father of the race, must be confessed a "hell-deserving sinner," and lying on the brink of eternal damnation as soon as it lies on its nurse's lap, then every man of sound moral feeling is entitled to protest against a doctrine of which such a cruel absurdity is a necessary postulate.

This brings us to another stone of stumbling,

which the Christian doctors have set up, and which still remains as a very ugly porter to many persons standing at the gate of the house which is called Beautiful, and barring a kindly entrance. I mean, of course, the doctrine of eternal punishments. The ancient Greeks also taught this doctrine; but they taught it in a very modified form, as any one may see in the sixth book of Virgil, or in the more detailed descriptions of his great predecessor in that teaching—the philosopher Plato:—

> "Sedet, æternumque sedebit,
> Infelix Theseus."
>
> "Discite justitiam moniti, et non temnere divos."

Only a few flaming offenders were condemned to this state of hopeless reprobation and inexhaustible torture; and besides, as part of a theology not laid down in rigid propositions, but floating loosely in the shape of traditional fancies, such things could be stated in books, without giving any great offence to serious thinkers. They quietly pushed this and other offensive matters aside, and clung to what was good and profitable. But the Christian churches, unfortunately, cannot do so. They have committed themselves to a theology, drawn up by scholastic persons, in a series of formal propositions which challenge contradiction and refuse compromise. Therefore, the doctrine of infinite torture for finite sins is still stoutly maintained as a point of Christian faith, and as stoutly disowned by a large class of benevolent and thoughtful persons, who look upon such a doctrine as utterly inconsistent with the conception of a wise and benevolent Being.* Now, if there was not a great deal of dogmatic obstinacy, a fair amount of hermeneutical ignorance, and a considerable vein of cowardice also in the ecclesiastical mind, this stumbling-block might easily be removed. It does not require any very profound scholarship to know that the word *αἰώνιος*, which we translate *everlasting*, does not signify eternity absolutely and metaphysically: but only popularly, as when we say that a man is an eternal fool, meaning only that he is a very great fool. Biblical interpreters also ought to bear in mind, which they constantly seem determined rather to forget, that the Scriptures are not written in the style of a metaphysical or curiously-scientific treatise; but the language throughout is essentially popular, and perhaps necessarily with somewhat of that vagueness which

* J. S. Mill's Autobiography, chap. ii. Read also Childers' Pali Dictionary, article NIBBANAM, where he compares the Buddhist *annihilation* with the Christian *damnation*—not to the advantage of the latter.

characterises colloquial language as contrasted with the style of a professorial lecture, or a scientific definition.

Another stumbling-block which theologians have laid in the way of the devotees of physical science, is the CREATION OUT OF NOTHING. This dogma, which, as every scholar knows, is not necessarily contained in any place, whether of the Old or New Testament, arose in the Jewish Church, and has been stamped with orthodox authority in Christendom, partly from a pious desire to magnify the Divine Omnipotence, partly from the timid stupidity of clinging to the letter, instead of breathing the spirit of Scripture; and partly also from the evil trick which we have just mentioned of importing metaphysics and scholastic definitions into the Bible, from which all the Scriptures are the furthest possible removed. Now the objection to this doctrine on the part of modern thinkers I conceive to be this—that, though not perhaps absolutely impossible, it is contrary to all known experience, and highly improbable, if we are to judge of the constitution of things from what we see, not from what we choose to imagine. It is the vulgar imagination which delights to represent the Supreme Being as a sort of omnipotent harlequin, launching the fiat of his volition, as the nimble gentleman in the pantomime strikes the table with his wand, and out comes a man, or a monkey, or something else, out of nothing. This is man's crude conception; but God's ways are not as man's ways: and his way is EVOLUTION. Nothing is created out of nothing; and mere volition, even of an omnipotent Being, cannot be conceived as bringing into existence a thing of an absolutely opposite nature, called matter. What we see everywhere in us and above us, and around us, simply is, that the present grows out of the past, as the future grows out of the present. Growth, therefore, necessary and essential growth, by inherent reasonable force, is the proper expression of the great Divine fact of the universe. To us dependent ephemeral creatures, all existence is a Divine miracle; and the continuity of that Divine miracle in the shape of what we call growth is, so far as we can see, the eternal form of the Divine creativeness. The absolute dualism of mind and matter which is implied in the received orthodoxy of the Church, is not warranted by any fact that exact science can recognise; nowhere do we find mind acting without a material instrument, nowhere matter absolutely divorced from the action of inherent forces, inasmuch as even the most motionless statical condition of things most solid is always produced by a balance of forces in some way or other—forces which, if they are not blind, but acting according to a calculated law, as they manifestly do, are only another name for Mind. This view of the constitution of the universe, though quite familiar to the wisest of the ancient Greeks, when propounded in the face of our orthodox Christian theology, is generally disowned with a certain pious horror as Pantheism, a word to which a great chorus of thoughtless and ill-informed people are straightway ready to echo back, Atheism—with the feeling that the two terms, though etymologically as opposed as white and black, are practically the same. Now the religious world here is evidently confounding two very different things under a common name, as the word Sophist, for instance, through the shifting phases of more than two thousand years of a literary life, has been used to denote the most varied types of the intellectual man, from the profoundest thinker to the shallowest quibbler. Pantheism, scientifically understood, has nothing to do either with materialism or with atheism. It is opposed to Bitheism or to Dualism, and simply denies the existence of two opposite entities in the world of Divine reality, while it asserts the existence of only one. The world is essentially one; and the All, though externally many, is, when traced to its deepest roots, not different from the One; as the human body, for instance, is both one and many; the fingers, which are five, belonging nevertheless to the unity of the hand; and the upper and lower extremities, though four, belonging in the same way to the essential unity of the body. The term Pantheism, therefore, is not opposed to unity, or to the principle of unity in the world, which is God; and a Pantheist, as Hegel well said of Spinoza, may more properly be said to deny the world, than to deny God. It is possible, however, for a Pantheist to be such a one-sided creature as not to perceive the central unity which binds the cosmos into a grand organized whole. He may look only at the outside of appearances, and see nothing but an infinite drift and jostle and jabble of unreasoned atoms, producing, in some blind, utterly inexplicable fashion a thing on which we impose an imaginary unity by the use of the term universe. In this case the pantheist becomes what is usually called a materialist, or an atheist of the most hopeless and incurable class. But whoever holds by the two poles of actual existence—the ἕν and the πᾶν of the Greeks—or the centre and the periphery, if the analogy of a circle may seem to suit better—this pantheist, by whatever name he may be called, simply denies dualism, and asserts the co-essential and co-eternal necessary existence of the internal and the external, the one and the many, in the constitution of the universe. His theory affects only the nature of the bond which binds together the outside and the inside of the All. If, according to Dr. Paley's analogy taken literally, the world may by a mechanical generation have sometimes been conceived as a watch made by a watchmaker, according to the pantheistic way of looking at things the world might be called an animal —θεῖον ζῶον, as Plato, we remember, has it, in the concluding sentence of the "Timæus." Nor will it do to say that a man who is a pantheist, even in the best sense, must necessarily deny religion, because his theory destroys human personality, and denies individual responsibility, on the foundation of which all human society, as well as all religious obligation, is constituted. Freedom, personality, and responsibility are facts which no theological or metaphysical theories can meddle with, any more than they can with generation, or appetite, or digestion. The charge of annihilating individual responsibility can be brought against Calvinism with as much and as little justice as against Spinozism. The answer to all such speculative objections from transcendental theories, when brought into the world of practice, is a fact and a flogging: somewhat in the style that we read of Zeno the Stoic, who, like Calvin, was a great predestinarian, and on one occasion, being about to flog his slave for an act of theft, had his philosophy thrown abruptly in his face, with the apology—"Yes, master, I did steal the article; but I could not help it: it was ordained." To which the philosopher calmly replied:—"Yes; but it was ordained also that whoso steals shall be flogged!"

The offence given by theologians to reasonable men, when they set themselves in an authoritative and oracular style to interpret the Divine procedure, and to point out what pious people call "judgments," is so manifold that it would require a whole chapter to tell off even the heads of its multiplied absurdity. The general principle that lies at the bottom of all these false readings of Providence may be described as a tendency to look at every manifestation of Divine energy that falls under our eye in the light of human interests, and from the narrow human point of view only. This is an element which plays a prominent part in all early mythologies; and we shall deceive ourselves very much indeed, if we imagine that it plays no part in our sermons and our books of godly edification now. And yet if we consider the magnitude of the mundane system, and the complexity of the spheral relations, we ought to perceive that few things can be more absurd than to imagine that a terrible thunderstorm, for instance, or a swell of the waters in Morayshire or the Sandwich Islands, or a failure in the potato crop, must necessarily have something to do with the follies or the faults of some person or persons who may suffer from such calamities. Generally speaking we may say, that the discomfort which any individual creature may at any time suffer in the course of his career from the general arrangements of Providence, affords not the slightest ground for his looking on these discomforts as having any special personal reference to himself. It is different, of course, with evil which arises in our own little world, both the cause and the cure of which may oftentimes be sufficiently patent. If a man drink half-a-dozen glasses of strong spirits, and lose the use of his legs to-day, and find an unpleasant throbbing in his temples to-morrow, this is "a judgment" which he may interpret, without presumption, and with great profit. But if an invasion of woes and a prostration of all prosperity should overtake him, such as that which overwhelmed the patriarch Job, then let him read that wonderful old theological drama carefully, and learn to hold his tongue, and to withhold his counsel in the presence of the Most High. Man may know many things, but he has no vocation to set up as an interpreter-general of the Divine procedure, whether in reference to himself or to his fellow-men. I say it with sorrow; but there is in a certain class of pious books a great deal too much of this theological interpretation of circumstances, as if God were doing everything in the large scheme of his varied universe specially with reference to "the frames and feelings" of a petty individual, of no more consequence in the system of things than the single ant of a single ant-hill in the economy of a large forest. Answers to prayer in the biography of pious persons are often as ridiculous as interpretations of judgments are presumptuous. If there is not the slightest reason to conclude that those on whom the Tower of Siloam fell were greater sinners than those on whom it fell not, and, if they justly got an evasive answer who asked whether this man sinned or his parents that he was born blind, as little right have you to conclude that a pound-note, which came to you from an unknown hand through the Post-office, at the moment when you were at the point of need for it, came to you by special Divine interposition because you had that morning poured forth a particularly fervent prayer. All these "interpositions" and "interferences" are the product of a devout conceit, that can be satisfied with nothing less in the way of religion than such a constant display of petty preferences as a spoiled child receives from a partial mamma. The idea of a God constantly interfering in answer to prayer, or otherwise, is one of the most anthropomorphic of all theological conceptions. God cannot be said to "interfere," with the general order of Providence, any more than the steam can be said to interfere with the regular motions of the steam-engine. He who is everywhere the spring of all motion, and the source of all vital energy, cannot be supposed to be called out of his way to answer any invocator's particular need. If the wind is blowing west, it blows west from a Divine necessity in the harmonious currents of the atmosphere, which can no more be changed by your wanting it to blow east, than Niagara can stop its swell because you have thoughtlessly cast your shallop upon its sweep. Those who wish to pray with a reasonable piety, to which no atheism can object, will find in the Lord's prayer, or in the prayer of Socrates, a model which cannot be excelled: but rewards and punishments for violated law lie deeply seated in the general system of the All-wise government, and will not be evoked by any special application even of the most pious. For theology of this puerile description, Homer must be quoted as an authority, not Paul. The Christian Jove neither launches special thunderbolts to strike the heads of special offenders, nor prepares sugar-plums for the good boys and girls of the grand State church or the unrecognised conventicle.

Let no man imagine we are unwarrantably hard on the religious world, when we mention these things. The religious world is just as liable as any other world to the general human weakness of sliding into a caricature of itself, and presenting these distorted features for general admiration as a correct likeness. Besides, it is of the very nature of a high ideal to be unattainable, to admit only of approximation; and one of the highest compliments that can be paid to Christianity is that, when purely presented, it is apt to seem a great deal too good for the creatures to whom it is addressed. And, so far as our present purpose is concerned, looking upon the profession of atheism, even in the modified form of agnosticism, as a monstrosity in the moral history of the world, explicable only on the theory of reaction or revulsion from certain abusive and offensive aspects of Christianity in these times, we cannot exonerate ourselves from the necessary work of marshalling forth these abuses and offences in all their nakedness. A few still remain, not of a doctrinal, but of an ethical, social, or æsthetical character, which we shall now shortly allude to. First there comes asceticism and monkery—a very sad and lamentable chapter in the history of the Church, and which, in so far as it has triumphed, completely wipes out the grand practical distinction between Christianity and Buddhism. Whatever we know not about Buddha, one thing certainly we do know, that he commenced with being a licentious person and a voluptuary, and ended in the character of a mendicant monk; and succeeded—as indeed Brahmanism did in a considerable measure before him—in impressing this ridiculous type of an unnatural and unsocial sanctity as a model for human admiration from the Ganges to the Amoor. It is needless to say that a religion which declares war against the fundamental instincts of human nature must always fail, equally on the one side in regulating the passions of the thoughtless many, and on the other in commanding the suffrages of the thoughtful few. The principle of all asceticism is not to regulate, but to extirpate; but, though the masses may stare at the man who does violence to all his natural instincts, under the name of piety, and rends his flesh to prove the strength of his will, they will never be induced to follow his example; and as for the few persons who give themselves up to speculation on the principles of human action whom the world calls philosophers, whatever name they may bear, like the poets they have only one test by which they measure all things—NATURE. If it be contrary to man's nature that he should live like a mere pig, or a tiger, or any form of brute beast, it is equally contrary to his nature not to like a good dinner, and to shrink from a glass of good wine. Philosophy recognises no virtue in walking with peas in a man's shoes, or quarrelling with the butter on a man's toast. It is perfectly true that in all enjoyment, whether of wine or of butter-toast, there is a certain element of danger; the *too much* is always at hand, and chiefly in the very acme of pleasant excitement, to turn the sublime of enjoyment into the ridiculous or the low. In this view there is always safety in abstinence; but there is also weakness—weakness, and cowardice, and meagreness and poverty of spirit, and an offence against nature so gross, that the very aspect of it is enough to tempt a man to rush into its opposite. I, for one, can never look upon these sallow saints perusing skulls, and gazing up into Heaven through the narrow window-slits of a dark cell, which you see on the walls of all our great picture-galleries, without feeling myself driven for relief into a heathenish sympathy with a brawny Hercules, a blooming Venus, or a rubicund Dionysus. Always and everywhere enjoyment is natural; abstinence, self-mortification, and self-crucifixion in every shape (except by way of training for some special purpose, as in the case of the Greek athletes), abnormal, monstrous, inhuman, and absurd. And yet in the Lives of the Saints, and elsewhere, this purely negative, pedantic, and ridiculous sort of virtue is set up before the Church to admire, as the ideal of the highest excellence to which human nature can attain. As reasonably might a flower avoid the sun for fear of being burnt up, as a man forswear enjoyment for fear of falling into vice. A certain amount of peril is the price which we pay for all pleasure; and whoso for fear of the peril refuses the pleasure, must sit at a smoky fireside, or in a dank cell, and rot his life away in a spiritual or a carnal mouldiness—in either case stupidly.

We have neither monks nor nuns in Great Britain just now, I believe, of the stupid kind which Buddha in the East, and the Romanists of the Middle Ages, perched upon the platform of a false ideal. Our nuns are mere sisters of charity, who devote themselves to deeds of active benevolence, and wear a certain funereal dress more by the way of protection against rude insult than from any worship of death, or perverse conceit of unnatural mortification. To such a withdrawal from the bustle and whirl of common life into a quiet corner for a special rational purpose there can be no objection; only let not such persons imagine that they are more holy than their secular sisters, who allow themselves to browse at large on the broad common of the world without any artificial restrictions.

Perhaps they are more pure and more philanthropic: perhaps they are only more narrow and more meagre. But in some parts of these islands, especially the north-west of Scotland, we have a school of sombre religionists and black prophets, who, though not professedly monks, make their boast of a certain artificial gloomy piety and morose morality, which leads by direct revulsion into sensuality, irreligion, and practical atheism. Our newspaper columns and anecdote-books are full of strange stories about ministers and men infected with this dismal superstition. Mr. Buckle, who, for some time, passed for a great philosopher, was of opinion that this lowering Calvinism of the north was the natural product of the savage bens of West Ross-shire, and the frowning crags of Glencoe: a theory unfortunately rendered suspicious by the fact that Calvinism was born in Picardy, not in Poolewe or Ballachulish, and that the original Calvin in Geneva was as stern a disciplinarian, and as far removed from Luther's idea of the model man "who loves wine, women, and song," as any Macdonald or McIntosh beneath the Grampians. But whatever the cause may be, the fact undoubtedly remains. There is a class of Christian ministers in the Scottish Highlands, specially amongst the clergy of the Free Church, who declare openly that dancing, and singing, and cards, and theatres are deadly sins, and whosoever has anything to do with such amusements must be looked upon as the servant of the devil, and in danger of everlasting damnation. It would appear as if these persons wished to change all the brightness of the moral world into the similitude of their own bleak moors and black bogs, with no sound but the melancholy cry of the pewit, the whistling of the cold wind, or the drizzle of the persistent rain. Or it might perhaps seem that they wished to hold in their own hands a despotic monopoly of all vital utterances and all moral manifestations of the human creature: no music, but the long-drawn drone of their melancholy psalm-tunes; no meetings, but prayer-meetings; no eloquence, but the alternate whine and screech of their own sepulchral sermons. One must speak not mincingly about these gospellers, because they unquestionably do as much as human beings can do to drive all healthy-minded persons out of the bosom of the Church and into the bosom of Mr. Atkinson and Miss Martineau, and any kindly devotees of the agnostic persuasion who may spread their arms to receive them. The airs of solemn authority assumed by these persons in remote districts where they have no one to contradict them, are almost incredible. One of them, I have been informed, in a district of the wide county of Inverness, wishing to abolish merry meetings and dances of every kind in his parish, and knowing that a fiddle or some musical instrument was a necessary adjunct of such assemblies, took occasion one day, when her husband, who was a fiddler, happened to be absent, to call on a woman of his congregation, in order to give her a serious remonstrance on the grave sin of fiddling at balls and weddings. The woman confessed that it was not exactly the most saintly occupation, but she did not see there was any harm in it; that even King David, the man after God's own heart, danced before the Lord, which he could not have done without a fiddle, or some such instrument; and besides that, her husband might often earn a pound in the half year by his fiddling, which could not be well wanted when the rent was to be paid. "Well," said the minister, "here's a pound for you, and give me the fiddle." The woman obeyed: she brought down the fiddle and pocketed the pound, and the reverend gentleman forthwith broke the back of the instrument with a violent bang upon the table, and flung the wreck of it into the fire. This was dramatic enough ; but the fiddle was not yet exterminated. The woman, true to her descent from Eve, had, on this trying occasion, encountered the clerical bear with a touch of the wisdom of the serpent. She had brought down an old obsolete fiddle from the garret, and left the real offender unharmed in his case !

There is one special point in which Scottish Christianity stands on its point of honour, and which, of course also, plays a prominent part in the grave religiosity of these trans-Grampian Pharisees ; we mean the observance of the Sabbath ; an observance in the main highly commendable, and to be looked on with pride, as one of those fountains from which Scotsmen draw that calm strength and moral seriousness which makes them so efficient and so reliable in the earnest work of the world, wherever they are found. But there is undeniably a superstitious Judaical and anti-Christian element in the notions of these Highland ministers about the sabbath, which must be openly condemned, and practically contradicted on all occasions, because it tends to make religion both disagreeable and ridiculous. We have reason to believe that in most Highland families no minister's daughter would venture to touch the piano on Sunday, even to play psalm tunes: and in most parts of Scotland, very few clergymen have courage enough to show themselves outside of their garden wall on that day. I have known the case of a landlady in a civilised town, who dismissed a lodger because he sung hymns to the piano on the Lord's day, and gave her house an ill-name. A religion which thus commends itself to the notice of the world by the unnatural repression of healthy emotion, and the sympathetic culture of a stupid seriousness, need not be surprised, if in the biographies of not a few notable persons it finds itself enumerated among the agencies that led to perilous flirtations with various kinds of latitudinarianism, and then clean away into the hostile ranks of No-Church.

Two points of offence more, and we have done. England has seen, in these latter days, in the matter of sacerdotal claims, and ceremonial mummeries, a phenomenon to make the stars blush. There is, and can be, no such thing as a priesthood in Christianity: the Egyptians had a powerful hierarchy, and so had the Jews; the caste system of the Brahmans was another variety of the same rigid form of social organization; but the character of Christianity is essentially popular, personal, and democratic, and knows nothing of privileged orders, much less of persons with thaumaturgic virtue in their right hands, and a magical power in their touch. This is a phenomenon that belongs partly to the vulgarest phases of Heathenism, and partly is a stupid importation of Judaism into Christianity, which deprives it of its essentially humanitarian character, and confounds it with all that is most puerile and trifling in the practice of the lowest superstitions. In Christianity the congregation is the Church; the people are the priests; and the prayers and praises of the saints are the incense. St. Peter taught this distinctly in a public letter eighteen hundred years ago (1 Pet. ii. 5), but his successors in Rome slid rapidly into a total forgetfulness of the truth; and the high-church party in the English Church at the present moment seem emulously bent on showing whether they will do the greater insult to the religion which they profess by the insolence of their churchly claims, the puerility of their devotional services, or the narrowness of their human sympathies. If religion is to consist in a marshalled array of antic observances, postures, genuflexions, bowings, dresses and decorations, and all sorts of prescribed externalities, by all means let us raise the ancient Greeks from the dead, to help us at least to do the thing naturally and gracefully. But a man who has any smack of the New Testament must know how very far this curious concern about ecclesiastical mumming is from the mind of Christ, and from the soundness of apostolic teaching. "Let all things be done decently and in order!" is the wise precept of the great apostle, in regard to the external arrangements of sacred worship; but to make a conscience of any mere outward show and paraded symbolism, is to run right in the teeth of the great text which, applied to our times, simply says, that in Christ Jesus there is neither priest nor presbyter, nor High Church, nor Low Church, nor attitudinarian, nor latitudinarian, but a new creature.

The other offence with which we conclude this bill of indictment against Churches and Churchmen, is of a political nature. The Churchman, it was written long ago by the great poetical moralist, is a creature "fond of power." Well, he has great power naturally by virtue of the great human instinct of reverence which he represents; and, if to this power, which belongs to his spiritual office, there be added great worldly dignity, a more than average share of the good things of this life, and perhaps an honoured place in the supreme counsel of the nation, in all this there is nothing wrong, or rather a great good, if a society be otherwise well managed and justly balanced; nevertheless, as things go, such a proud position of the clergy is not without danger to the Church, lest it should become worldly, and danger to religion, lest it should become identified with odious oligarchic privilege and selfish oligarchic exclusiveness. The democratic atheist is a species of the unlovely genus which we specified above; and there cannot be the slightest doubt that where, as in England, democracy as the form of the civil government is combined with sacerdotal glorification among the clergy, and a distinct aristocratic type in Church polity, the democratic atheist is an animal that will show front in large centres of civic life pretty confidently, and cast his volleys of ungracious denial into the sun's face, not without observance. This, of course, is not meant as any argument for the dis-establishment of any of the British Churches; it is merely noticed pathologically as helping to account for a moral disease, and an intellectual perversion more widely spread among certain sections of the working classes in our large towns than many persons are apt to imagine.

It remains now, in order to bring the matter to a more distinct and definite bearing, that we present the atheism or agnosticism of the present day before the reader in the words of its own advocates; that we may see how far their opinions are a mere illustration of the vulgar law of reaction; or how far anything like a substantial reason, sound logic, or subtle sophistry lies at the bottom of their abnormal speculations. If it should turn out, on coming face to face with the utterances of those negative philosophers, that there is really nothing more in what they urge than a hasty revulsion from the real or imaginary aberrations of the received orthodoxy, it will be at once a great confirmation to sound theism, and a vindication of human reason from one of its strangest aberrations. The folly or presumption of the unreasonably orthodox will appear to have supplied a provocation which has driven the reasonably heterodox into a position of which they would otherwise have been ashamed. Protagoras—one of the most notable of the ancient Greek sophists in the age of Pericles—commenced his most famous book on the principles of human knowledge, quite in the spirit of our modern agnostics in these words:

> "If there be gods,
> Or if there be not, overjumps my ken:
> But this I know—I am a man, and take
> Of things that be the measure for myself,
> And things that be not."

Now, if this most reputable of the sophists—for Plato paints him in the most favourable colours—meant by this famous sentence merely that he did not know whether Jove, Athena, and Apollo, as they were then conceived and worshipped by the Greeks, existed or not, and was determined, as a practical man, not to care, he said what no impartial thinker now can blame him for. But if he meant to say that he believed in no self-existent Divine power underlying these names, and saw no cause for supposing the existence of any such power, we should say he was a fool, or a man not to be dealt with reasonably, as not perceiving that a world everywhere full of reasonable construction could be supposed to come into existence, or to exist for ever, without a reasonable substratum. Exactly so with our modern agnostics. If we find that by the general term atheism or agnosticism they merely mean to deny certain popular conceptions about the Supreme Being, which they cannot believe, this is an intelligible position: they may be right or wrong in their notions; but their attitude is not unworthy of rational beings, and will be judged of more or less leniently by the impartial spectator, according to the greater or less amount of the provocation from the unreasonable orthodox which they may seem to have received. When, on the other hand, we find them flying off in a fit of hasty revulsion, and, from the prevalence of what they believe to be, and what may actually be, shallow, perverse, and altogether unworthy notions about the Supreme Being, concluding, at a jump, that there is no God, we can only pity the morbid sensibility of a temper which had the power to drive reasonable men into so unreasonable an attitude. Let us hear, therefore, what they have to say for themselves. First, Miss Martineau—or rather, her father in atheism, Mr. Atkinson—and then Professor Tyndall; for these are two of the most respectable, and whom the more coarse and rabid of the negative faction can only be benefited by accepting as their representatives.

MR. ATKINSON.

1. "Instinct, passion, thought, are effects of organized substances."—*Page* 6.

2. "For every effect there is a sufficient cause; and all causes

are material causes influenced by surrounding circumstances; which is nothing more than matter being influenced by matter." —*Page* 7.

3. "What use is there in disputing with a Mohammedan about his prophet, or his harem? or with the Roman Catholic about his saints and his transubstantiation? or with the English Protestant about his dull formalism, his services, and his worldly pride, and vulgar regard for wealth?"—*Page* 10.

4. "Mind is the product of the brain; it is the manifestation or expression of the brain in action."—*Page* 17.

5. "Before animal existence there were electric currents and aroma from vegetation, and solemn music from winds; then sentience was provided; and after more ages consciousness followed upon sentience."—*Page* 26.

6. "It is only knowledge of the laws of mind and the law of love, and exhibitions of goodness and mercy, that will reform the world. Inferior minds will, doubtless, always be influenced by rewards and punishments; but these rewards and punishments should be of a more wholesome character, and not such as brutalise, and encourage the selfish impulses. Preaching the horrors of a hell and eternal damnation will never induce reverence for higher things, or reform the world."—*Page* 136.

7. "We must profit by Bacon's admonitions, and not mix up theology with science; we must not see ourselves reflected—see the ghosts of ourselves in Nature, and imagine we recognise design or a human origin of things. We must follow our great master, Bacon, and make a stand against the fallacy of natural theology, and that exceedingly weak argument of Paley's about the watch, which only places the difficulty a little further off, and confounds the idea of creation with design or manufacture. To design is human. Men design by following the laws which constitute Nature."—*Page* 139.

8. "Ignorance sees Nature in parts, personifies effects, and takes them for causes. It creates horrors and spectres, and then startles at its own creations. Ignorance imagines gods and devils in legions. Knowledge establishes the true relations of things in a whole, and has only one God; and that incomprehensible and

unknown, and cannot admit a principle of Evil, much less a personal demon—an embodiment of all villainy; but, on the contrary, sees good in evil, and the working of general laws for the general good; and sees no more sin in a crooked disposition than in a crooked stick in the water, or in a hump-back, or a squint. Ignorance conceives its will to be free: a strange arrogance, if it could see it. Knowledge recognises universal law, and that nothing can be free or by chance—no, not even God; but that God is the substance of law, and origin of all things."—*Page* 141.

9. "There is a trinity in unity described by Bacon which seems to offer a sound commencement of philosophizing: matter, form, and the principle of motion, or the power or mind of Nature, if such expressions be preferred. . . . . All is change—change eternal. Motion is fundamental to the constitution of Nature; and the forms of matter and the condition of mind (which is one form of the properties of matter) are all passing phenomena, fleeting and various as the wind, equally determined by law, bound down by the adamantine chain of necessity. There is nothing stable but what we conceive to be fundamental to all these forms and changes, but which is beyond sense-impressions. We assume a something and a principle because the form of mind requires it, as a thing essential, though unknown; and it is this which I, wrongly enough, perhaps, termed God."—*Page* 170.

10. "Philosophy finds no God in Nature; no personal Being or Creator, nor sees the want of any."—*Page* 173.

11. "If men will make a fable for what is beyond our comprehension, let the poetry be sublime and worthy of the subject. Let the God be an ideal abstract of all that is unimpassioned, noble, and elevating; and, above all, let it be a mystery—not a thing carved in stone, or shaped out in blood and bone; a thing of human passion aud imperfections, fabricating that which it afterwards finds imperfect, and repenting of having made it."—*Page* 174.

12. "In Nature there can be no favouritism or predestination, though all things be fated as being according to law—law which rules impartially, though individuals suffer cruel extremities from necessity; all evil, however, having some tendency towards universal good, as manure and decaying matter are the substances essen-

tial to regeneration and the golden harvest. But men fancy that they recognise the doings of a mind like their own in Nature, instead of perceiving that they themselves are of a form cast from Nature, and a response to the surface or phenomenal form of things without. Thus deluding themselves, they wander after final causes, and by an inverted reason see their own image in Nature, and imagine design and a Designer—creation and a Creator; as if the laws of matter were not fundamental, and sufficient in themselves, and design were not human, and simply an imitation; or, as Bacon designates it, 'a memory with an application.' To call Nature's doings, and the fitness and form of things, design, is absurd. Man designs; nature is."—*Page* 175.

13. "What can be more noble and more glorious than a calm and joyful indifference about self and the future, in merging the individual in the general good, the general good in universal Nature? And what are all our creeds and conventionalities but empty vanities, a false show, the swaddling-clothes of children—the crutches on which decaying age, broken down by false stimulants, supports itself?"—*Page* 189.

14. "He is taught to respect this morality of vengeance and of partiality; that man can do no good of himself, and yet has a free will; and that the soul or life can be separated as an entity, and be independent of the living thing. He is taught that few are chosen to heaven, but the greater number to damnation; and this is to be considered a most consoling doctrine. And while men may be born to hell-fire, they are instructed to love God with all their hearts, and to forgive one another to the seventy times seven. Stimulated to selfishness by the idea of reward and punishment, they are required to be unselfish, and urged to set their hearts on high things. They are taught to believe that they could not have existed as a consequence of Nature, and as Nature; but that they were created by a Being resembling themselves, who is at the same time incomprehensible; that all nature is a fabric made out of nothing; but that this wondrous Being—the first cause, is himself without a cause or beginning. They are to consider it necessary that man should have a maker, but that the demand of causality is to rest there."—*Page* 204.

15. "From the recognition of universal LAW, we shall develop a universal LOVE. We shall see that no man can be a friend to us who is not a friend to all. We shall learn that dirt is beauty unformed, and that evil is undeveloped good."—*Page* 209.

16. "Men sing to the praise and glory of God, seeing in Him a jealous man, the wretched image of their own miserable selves."

17. "Though man cannot make the smallest worm or particle of dust, he imagines a Creator or Cause to be the same vain, incompetent animal as himself."—*Page* 227.

18. "Fitness in Nature is no evidence of design. That the lungs are fitted for breathing, and the eye for seeing, is no more evidence of design than that the seal is fitted to the impression, or that two halves make the whole."—*Page* 228.

19. "He who does not suppose a personal God or Lord for a future, may, nevertheless, be most unselfish and deeply religious—so religious, that he shrinks from all the forms of worship, because he sees in them all but forms of worship, and forms of fancy, and not the spirit and the image of truth. There are thousands upon thousands who have no clear knowledge on any one question relating to their religion, and yet are most proud in declaring themselves Christians, although it be not certain that they possess any one Christian self-denying virtue.

"Were Christ to appear among such persons, he would not be recognised; nor would he recognise them as Christians. Saying, 'I am a Christian,' and crying, 'Lord! Lord!' will not open the gate of heaven to any man; and those who would jostle in before their neighbours shall be the last to enter and the least in heaven,—in the heaven of a truly virtuous and loving heart. I think a man may be so religious as to be quite shocked with all notions of prayer and all familiar intercourse with deity whatsoever. We must pause in wonder before the great mystery of Nature, the hidden truth and the cause, and learn that knowledge is power, and knowledge is wisdom, and wisdom and power are in obedience; for, by yielding to this law, the law is fulfilled, and the works are accomplished. Christ lived and died for the good of mankind; Socrates lived and died for the good of mankind; and so ought we all to live and die for the good of mankind; and only by forgetting self shall we elevate and ennoble life. I would not accept of heaven if I thought that others were to go to hell."—*Page* 229.

20. "Christian morals are considered perfect; but they will require much weeding and developing before they can be accepted by high and philosophic minds—by the best and most enlightened minds of the present day. And is there no place for man's faith when he has ceased the worship of idols? It is the idlest folly to suppose that the idea of Necessity would let men loose among their evil passions. But, that we require something to reverence and elevate our thoughts towards, is true: knowledge gives us a more elevated poetry, gives us the chart and laws of mind to guide us, and will exhibit to us higher objects for reverence. Is it nothing to have faith in Nature; to have faith in knowledge, and in goodness, which is the fruit of knowledge? Is it nothing to have faith in love? Is it nothing to regard Nature in all her forms with profound reverence? to love truth and worship goodness, and find no place for contempt of any living thing or condition of matter? Trained in the knowledge of the laws of mind, to find it impossible to take offence; what a soothing influence! What a blessing this one circumstance! What a foundation for virtue and generosity! and for peace of mind! Is it nothing to cast away ambition? to desire excellence rather than to excel? to feel a noble contentment in reflecting that you are a part of Nature—a form of the eternal? Is there nothing in that faith which seeks for happiness out of self in the happiness of others, and the glories of N ture—content that in death the lease of personality shall pass away, and that you shall be as you were before you were—in a sleep for evermore?"—*Page* 230.

21. "I am far from being an atheist, as resting on second causes. As well might we, resting on this earth, deny that there is any depth beneath, or, living in time, deny eternity. I do not say, therefore, that there is no God: but that it is extravagant and irreverent to imagine that cause a Person. All we know is phenomena; and that the fundamental cause is wholly beyond our conception. In this I do not suspend my judgment; but rather

assert plainly that of the motive power or principle of things we know absolutely nothing, and can know nothing: that no form of words could convey any knowledge of it; and that no form of thought could imagine that which is wholly aside of Nature (as Nature is to us), and of the nature of the mind, and, as it were, behind the understanding. A 'cause of causes' is an unfathomable mystery. Phenomena necessarily have a certain form and order which we term law. The most fundamental and general law is what Bacon terms Forms. I cannot believe in a manufacturing God, as implied in the idea of a Creator and a creation; nor can I believe in any beginning or end to the operations of Nature. The cause in Nature or of Nature is eternal and immutable. The earth and stars may pass away into other forms; but the law is eternal —man, animals, plants, stones are consequently in Nature. The mind of man, the instincts of animals, the sympathies (so to speak) of plants, and the properties of stones, are results of material development; that development itself being a result of the properties of matter, and the inherent cause or principle which is the basis of matter. If to have this conception of things is to be an atheist, then am I an atheist. If to renounce all idolatry, and to repose upon the deep and solemn conviction of an eternal and necessary cause—such a Cause as that, with our faculties, we could not know, or, as it is expressed, 'could not see and live'—if this be atheism or materialism, be it so. I care not about terms."—*Page* 240.

22. "What is mind, but an evolved condition or form of the powers of Nature, like light, heat, magnetism? What are the instincts of animals and the mind of man but a result of chemical action or material processes?"—*Page* 257.

23. "Perhaps in the end it may be seen that some of those that are called Materialists are the most spiritual in their notions: more spiritual, at least, than those who talk of gross materialism, and at the same time invoke their material God, who sits upon a throne; who talk disparagingly of human affections, and human wisdom, and poor human nature, and at the same time fashion their God in their likeness."—*Page* 259.

MISS MARTINEAU.

24. "When men are driven out of their grosser superstitions by the evidence of LAW. which are everywhere around them, they still cling to the baseless notion of a single conscious Being outside of Nature, himself unaccounted for, and not himself accounting for Nature."—*Page* 218.

25. "When we have finally dismissed all notion of subjection to a superior lawless Will—all the perplexing notions about sin and responsibility, and arbitrary reward and punishment—and stand free to see where we are, and to study our own nature, and recognise our own conditions—the relief is like that of coming out of a cave full of painted shadows under the free sky, with the earth open round about us to the horizon. What a new perception we obtain of 'the beauty of holiness'—the loveliness of a healthful moral condition—accordant with the laws of Nature, and not with the requisitions of theology! What a sense of reverence awakens in us when, dismissing the image of a Creator bringing the universe out of nothing, we clearly perceive that the very conception of origin is too great for us, and that deeper and deeper down in the abysses of time, further and further away in the vistas of the ages, all was still what we see it now—a system of ever-working forces, producing forms uniform in certain lines and largely various in the whole, and all under the operation of immutable Law!"—*Page* 219.

26. "I am convinced that the true moral life is found in going out of ourselves."—*Page* 222.

We have presented these extracts at considerable length from a conviction that no other method could be so effectual in showing the emptiness, absurdity, and self-contradictory nature of all arguments that can be advanced in favour of the monstrous doctrine of atheism. Part of the affair is a mere logomachy arising from a strange use of words; another part is an impatient recalcitration against certain doctrines of the received theology of the Christian Churches, or of the theology of certain ignorant and foolish vain talkers in Christian pulpits and books of Christian devotion; a third part is an exaggeration of the vices of Christians, and a glorification of the virtues of atheists; and the rest of it is a conglomeration of misunderstandings and cross-purposes which resists all attempt at being brought within the pale of a reasonable logic. Let us take it with all briefness in detail.

REMARKS.

NOS. 1, 2, 4, 5, 22. To bring any sense out of these propositions we shall require a new definition of MATTER. If matter is made to include *motion*, both secondary motions and that primary source of all energy "in whom we live, and MOVE, and have our being," then of course we may say with all truth that everything in the world is only matter influencing matter. But it would be equally true to adopt Spinoza's language and to say that everything in the world is only God influencing God. But what sense is there in inverting the common acceptation of known terms, and then tricking out a philosophy from such perversion of language? It was in this way that Bentham got himself a certain temporary reputation as a moralist, by confounding the good with the pleasurable.* There can be no speculative error, though unquestionably a most uncalled-for amount of practical confusion, in substituting the word MATTER for God, provided we import into our idea of matter all those transcendental virtues, energies, and functions which the theist recognises as inherent in the great First Cause. But why this juggle? Far more reasonable were it to deny the existence of matter altogether, than to attribute to it qualities plainly inconsistent with its fundamental conceptions.

When it is said that "the mind is the product of the brain," this is just as true as to say that the horse is the product of the cart. No doubt brain and thought are indissolubly bound together—as we might conceive horse and cart to be—but as both mind and brain are products of the inherent self-energizing, self-plastic Mind of the universe,

* That Bentham's ethical system is utterly worthless, was afterwards confessed by his principal disciple. See J. S. Mill's "Essay on Bentham."

which we call God, it is quite unwarranted to call the one the product of the other. They are both products of God; or, if you dislike the word products, say manifestations, emanations, or evolutions. Behind all such phrases God lies as necessarily as the sun behind the radiance which he sheds.

To the doctrine of EVOLUTION enunciated in No. 5 there can be no objection, provided always that we do not assert the absurdity that something is evolved out of nothing, reason out of unreason, order out of confusion, light out of darkness, fire out of frost, or the positive in any shape out of mere blind negations. In all such cases only the most superficial will confound a historical sequence, or an accidental priority, with a metaphysical priority, or a Cause.

No. 3. The faults and follies of professing Christians have no more logically to do with Christianity than the errors made by schoolboys in summing up an arithmetical column with the principles of the science of number.

In No. 6 there is a confusion between the conferring of rewards and acting for the sake of obtaining rewards. The interpolation of the selfish motive of course corrupts the purity of the action;

but it is not therefore wrong to reward those who, from unselfish regards, have sacrificed themselves for the good of the community.

No. 7. Bacon is quite right when he tells us not to mix up theology with science; but he would be altogether wrong, if he were to tell us not to mix up theology with philosophy. Science works in a narrow range, and has no function to meddle with philosophical or theological questions at all. The question of design is a philosophical question, and the moment a scientific man either asserts it or denies it, he walks out of his proper sphere, and is, or attempts to be, a philosopher. As for Dr. Paley, and his simile of the watch, no writer that I know has been more grossly abused and made to stand a more unreasonable test in the literal interpretation of his words. Dr. Paley—the genius of common-sense, as he has been well called—did not say, and did not in the remotest degree mean to insinuate, that the world is a watch, or a manufacture in any shape. He merely said that as we see and acknowledge design, plan, purpose, and calculation in the machinery of a watch, so, unless we are altogether ignorant and purposely perverse, we must acknowledge design, plan, calculation, purpose, in the structure of the human body, and in other organisms of Nature; and this doctrine, expounded more than two thousand years ago by Socrates, the wisest of the Greeks, and besung by David, the noblest of the Hebrew lyrists, is so strikingly and pervadingly true that no subtleties and sophistries and wretched verbal juggleries of a purely negative physical science can hope to overturn it. We do not require the atheists or agnostics to tell us that Nature is a growth, not a manufacture; that God is not a mechanic, and so forth; we know this perfectly well—we happen to have been taught, as Christians, that God is a Spirit, and a spirit in whom we live, and move, and have our being; but a growth, to rise into any congruous proportions, requires design, as well as a box, or a house, or any piece of mechanical compagination. "Man *designs*, Nature *is*," says Mr. Atkinson. This is an antithesis merely in words, which to a thinking mind conveys no meaning. The writer should have said, Man MAKES; Nature IS: though, indeed, in the proper sense, man does not even make; he only uses what is. But neither in the making, nor the using, nor the being, is there the slightest reason for the exclusion of design. Design belongs, and must belong, to all the three; otherwise every human workshop would become a lumber-room of incoherent fragments, and instead of a world everywhere full of reasonable law, we should have a lawless chaos and a maundering Bedlam. The prejudice against design in the minds of a certain class of scientific men arises from two causes—1. Because mere science does not mount up into the region of final causes, and therefore takes upon itself to deny generally what, for its own special purposes, it does not require; 2. Because some foolish theologians have interpreted a design into certain parts of the Divine workmanship, which a little knowledge of the scheme of Nature proved to be altogether inadequate; and 3. Because the design which we admire in the scheme of Nature is part of a plan comprehending a vast whole, not to be interpreted by the hasty inspection of a part; and those who expatiate largely on the final cause of the part as if it were the whole, and look at this part also only in the light of human convenience and comfort, are justly chargeable with ignorance and presumption. God certainly does not do all that he does in this vast and complex universe merely for your pleasure or mine; nor because you and I can make profitable application of anything in the world does it logically follow that this use was in every case an end, and not rather an accident of their existence; but unquestionably he is a most blind person who does not see, and a most ungracious person who does not acknowledge, as Socrates says, that the gods have done a very great deal to make human beings as comfortable as possible. As to what Mr. Atkinson says, that fitness of parts does not prove design, because the fact that two halves make a whole may not prove design; the answer is plain, that not every adaptation or congruity proves design, but only such a combination of diverse means to a common end as is absolutely impossible to conceive without the directing presence of that imperial Unity which we call Mind. Break a bridge in two, and join the two halves together again. You say this does not indicate design. But did the bridge, as a skilful junction of stones, bars, or boards to connect two banks of a river, put itself together without design? or could even the two halves of a bridge, or of any other body, have fitted so exactly into a whole, if there had not been a shaping and moulding power behind the materials, to shape them into such a whole? Let us not therefore say, there is no τέλος, design, or final cause in the works of God, while we admit that no meanest work of man can be without it; but let the manifest truth rather be stated thus: the designs of man are petty, partial, and dealing only with supplied materials; the design of God is one, pervading, inherent, self-acting, unavoidable. As thoughts are in the mind of a great poet, always shaping themselves out by constructive reason and intuitive design into organic imaginative structures called poems, so the eternal ideas in the Divine mind are always shaping themselves forth by inherent, necessary, eternal, self-evolving, self-plastic Reason into those living poems of the creative intellect which we call worlds. With God every thought is a deed; and thoughts and deeds together evolved in the miraculous chain of vital continuity which we call growth are the essence of that incomprehensible, reasonable Source of all existence called GOD, which all pure religion devoutly worships, all sober philosophy piously acknowledges, and no subtle argumentation can explain away.

No. 8, 21. There is little here that a reasonable theist would be disposed to deny. The declaration "that God is the substance of Law, and the origin of all things," shows how difficult it was for Mr. Atkinson or any sound-minded man to maintain consistently the unreasonable negatives of pure atheism.

No. 9. Curiously and perversely enough, he here corrects himself for having used the term GOD, and thinks it safer to talk of a fundamental something beyond sense, and underlying all change. One can see nothing here, but an unreasonable and superstitious horror, against the use of a venerable name which has been sanctioned by all the noblest religions and all the loftiest philosophies that were assayed to give formulated utterance to the most deeply-seated instincts of human consciousness.

No. 10. The objection of modern devotees of physical science to "a personal God," seems to arise from their using the term person in the sense of *human* person. It is therefore identical with the objection to an anthropomorphic God, which from the days of Xenophanes downwards has been found in the van of all objections to the popular theology; but modern objectors should bear in mind that Christianity is not polytheism; and that the use of anthropomorphic phrases, even by the most spiritual Christian theologians on occasions, arises from a necessity of the human imagination, and does not in the least imply that the persons using such phrases think of Jehovah as the Greeks did of Jove. Scientific men are sometimes rather prosaic, and may be excused if they mistake a simile for a proposition; but philosophers, or persons propounding philosophical propositions, should know better. As to the objection to the term Creator, we have stated in a previous chapter that the production of something out of nothing, by a metaphysical causation is not taught formally in any text of the Christian Scriptures.

No. 12. The favouritism and predestination alluded to here is a vulgar misunderstanding of the Pauline doctrine of election, a doctrine which, as we have already stated, was taught by the ancient Stoics, and is founded on the soundest views of the general course of Providence. The doctrine of philosophical necessity is objectionable only when it denies the limited liberty which we plainly enjoy, or when it is stated, with the atheists, as a blind necessity or chance, not a seeing necessity of the living God.

No. 13. The extraordinary conception which lies at the root of this passage is, that because some Christians are selfish, therefore religion is essentially selfish, and because Mr. Atkinson, Miss Martineau, and other agnostics are benevolent persons, therefore the only way to infect the world with beneficence is to adopt the atheistical opinions of those persons!

No. 14. This is a fair average specimen of those oblique and perverse views of Christian ethics which are so common in the mouths of the agnostics. That they have received some provocation from foolish advocates and inconsistent professors, we have all along admitted; but, surely men professing to be wise above their fellows should not allow themselves to be led away by such hasty generalisations, and to see things with such distorted optics.

Nos. 15, 17. The word LAW is the last term with those who disdain to use the name of GOD, as the symbol of the underlying reasonable cause of the grand order of the universe. But this word, however fashionable, is utterly void of philosophical significance. A law is simply a regular method of operation, and implies either an internal or an external causal Force, whose constant and consistent action produces that method of operation. The motion of the piston in a steam-engine proceeds according to a law; but no sane man could dream of substituting that expression of regularity in the movement for the true cause of the movement. The cause of the law in this case is the nature of steam + the designing mind of James Watt. So with everything else: the men on a chess-board, the balls on a billiard-table, the soldiers in an ordered battle, move according to a law; but to substitute that law for the cause of these motions is unmeaning babble. The cause of all motion is a motive force; and the cause of all reasonable motion, or motion according to a law, is a reasonable motive force. And in this way the cause of the laws of Nature, which we are called upon to substitute for God, is the supreme designing Reason, or reasonable Force, which we call God, plus the nature of the materials which Divine Force uses in working the organism of the universe.

No. 20. There is not the slightest reason to deny that atheists and agnostics may lead most virtuous and noble lives, and may have their own special comfort from their own special creed. We only object to the easy egotism by which all the higher virtues are appropriated to the atheistic creed, and denied to the theistic.

No. 24. Here we have that phantom of "a single conscious Being, *outside* nature," which seems to have driven the atheistic mind of these times out of its proprieties. The conception of a Jupiter sitting outside of the world, either on the topmost peak of Olympus, is quite foreign both to philosophical theism and to spiritual Christianity; but, notwithstanding the plainest contradictions to the contrary, the obliquity of these people will rush off at the mere sound of an innocent imaginative expression, right away into the black negations of Law and Necessity, and atheism, or at least what they call an impersonal God. When theists call God a person, they certainly do not do so because they conceive him as a separate unit, bounded by the narrow limits of human personality, but because they deem it most suitable to describe the supreme cause of all nature by that which is most noble in nature. We know nothing higher in the visible world than personality; and nothing higher in the invisible than God. If by an impersonal God is meant, only a God freed from all limits of merely human personality, there is no great harm in it; but the phrase is extremely vague; and may mean something, or anything, or nothing at all. We shall therefore, wisely, have nothing to do with it. It may fill up the yawning vacuities of atheism, with some decency; otherwise worthless.

I have given this full consideration to the religious and theological opinions of Mr. Atkinson, not because I attribute, or have the slightest reason to attribute, any peculiar authority to his utterances, but because his words represent fairly enough that oblique vision, and distorted portraiture of Christian doctrine and morals, which, seasoned up with the favourite scientific phraseology of the hour, is cooked up into so many shallow shapes of more or less distinctly enunciated atheism. Of Miss Martineau specially, we have said nothing. Unquestionably she was a lady, not only of rare intellectual gifts, but with a moral nature of the most delicate sensibility; theologically, however, she was content to put herself before the world as the mere reflective mirror of Mr. Atkinson, and must stand or fall with him. We now turn to Professor Tyndall, a scientific expositor of much higher pretensions, and one from whose well-weighed words, placed before the British Association at Belfast in the year 1874, we may expect to gather with more precision the real sentiments of the materialists and agnostics of the present day. I have read his celebrated address over several times, with great care; and I have now little doubt as to its real significance and drift. It certainly does not announce an intellectual philosophy of nature; the prominence which it gives to the doctrine of atoms, and the favour shown to Democritus, Epicurus, and Lucretius, as compared with Plato, Aristotle, and Zeno, gives a decidedly atheistical or materialistic hue to the introductory paragraphs; but on the whole, the concluding sections and the general tone of the remarks in the body of the address incline me to conclude that the lecturer is a Pantheist, and who would have no objections to worship the God of Spinoza, Giordano Bruno, or Goethe, if he felt any movement in his soul towards worship at all. The concluding lines, indeed, from Wordsworth, which the learned gentleman has italicised, are distinctly Pantheistic,

> "A motion and a spirit that impels
> All thinking things, all objects of all thought,
> And rolls through all things"—

and one can hardly conceive a writer, sympathizing with Wordsworth at all, and at the same time dealing in the blank vacuities and barren negations of pure atheism. I have already explained that pantheism, so long as it asserts the unity of motion and spirit and mind in a reasonably-ordered universe, is a perfectly legitimate form of theism, to which not even orthodox Christianity, rightly understood, need have any serious objection. But there is a mist and a confusion and a slippery ambiguity about Professor Tyndall's phraseology which prevents the impartial reader from extracting all that joy from the final Wordsworthian quotation that it might otherwise naturally create. The very fact of placing Democritus, Epicurus, and Lucretius formally above Plato and Aristotle shows a want of something in the writer's philosophy which no quotations borrowed from writers of a more lofty school can supply. To reconcile Democritus and Wordsworth as we know them is impossible. I say *as we know them*, because we know Democritus only from fragments; and it may have been the case that the great father of the atomic doctrine, like Thales and the other wise pre-Socratic sages, had a *Λόγος*, or Reason, in the background, by the help of which his atoms might shape themselves into a reasonable universe. But as things now stand neither Epicurus, the expositor of Democritus, nor Lucretius, nor the modern scientific lecturer, makes any use of *Λόγος*, or *Νοῦς*, or any intellectual potency in their construction of the universe. It constructs itself by evolution, natural selection, laws, and a few other fashionable phrases, which, divorced from a self-existent, plastic *Λόγος*, or Reason, as we have already explained, to a thinking mind, have simply no significance at all. Of one thing Professor Tyndall seems wisely aware: if this sort of materialistic and agnostic talk is to go on, we must change our definition of the word MATTER; and, no doubt, if it is made to include motion, and not only blind motion, but reasoned motion, and motion according to a law, we may then say that Matter so gifted contains "the promise and potency of all terrestrial life." But, as we said with reference to Mr. Atkinson, why confound all reasonable discussion by using words in an entirely novel and self-contradictory sense? If matter includes motion, then matter + motion + form, the result of motion in a reasonable world, = GOD; and why not deny matter altogether, instead of elevating it into a position which it cannot consistently maintain? But letting this pass, we observe further that Professor Tyndall, no less than Mr. Atkinson, is pursued by the phantom of an external, mechanical, detached, and interfering God, of whose existence no sane Christian theist ever dreamed. Another man of straw against which he seems to be fighting is " a series of creative acts," as if it were at all necessary for any theist to believe in the existence of any such acts. Inasmuch as God is everywhere present, he must be everywhere and always energizing according to the necessity of his own eternal reason; and there is not, nor can there be conceived, any such thing as a want of continuity in the indwelling plastic energy by which he is constantly shaping forth the life of the universe. And Evolution, of which the learned lecturer also makes large discourse, is a doctrine to which no Christian theologian can have the slightest objection; unless, indeed, there be some divines who, taking the first chapter of Genesis in its literal signification—which only a prosaic person of the lowest order would do—imagine that God created the world by six verbal fiats, like the strokes of a harlequin, one in each of six days, and then retired from the scene, with nothing to do, as I have heard it sometimes expressed in the pulpit, but to "contemplate his own Infinite perfections!" Having dispensed as much as possible with the idea of a plastic MIND in the universe, and having assigned the natural functions of such plastic Mind to a newly baptized Matter, we are not to be surprised if Professor Tyndall goes on to magnify the famous shibboleth of the ingenious physical speculator, Dr. Darwin, and to employ "natural selection" to do the work which devout thinkers like Copernicus and Kepler have agreed with Moses, King David, and other prophets and wise men, in ascribing to God. The beauty of flowers, he tells us, is due to natural selection. Will he be so good as tell us whether, when a selection is made, it must not be made on some principle, which both renders the act of selection possible, and causes it to be made in a particular way? If the selection is made in the fashion that the stronger overwhelms and absorbs the weaker, in this case it is plain that there must be a principle of strength in nature which forces its way over weakness. To this doctrine no man of sense can object. But in the same way, if the selection takes place in the fashion that beauty prevails over ugliness, it can only be because there is a principle of beauty in nature that rejoices in its own propagation. Well, then, unquestionably there is such a principle in nature, otherwise how could the world everywhere be blooming and bursting with beauty, or at least tending towards beauty in some shape or other? But what is this principle? Professor Tyndall, unless he gives up Democritus and Epicurus, cannot answer this. Plato can. Beauty is the *Λόγος, Νοῦς*, or Mind, of the cosmos, manifesting itself in the delicately-shaped congruities of visual form. Hence the beauty of ferns and other leafy tracery. GOD IN ALL AND THROUGH ALL AND FOR ALL, is the only formula that can explain these things. Without God, evolution, continuity of nature, natural selection, conservation of energy, or whatever other phrases happen to have currency for the hour, are mere sound and smoke, and imaginations of science falsely so called.

THE END.